SMART MOUTHS

THE BEST QUOTATIONS EVER COLLECTED

by the Knowledge Commons

Ashland, Oregon

Instant Genius:
Smart Mouths

For information, write:
Portable Press
P.O. Box 1117, Ashland, OR 97520
www.portablepress.com • 888-488-4642

Cover design by Michael Brunsfeld, San Rafael, CA
(Brunsfeldo@comcast.net)

ISBN-13: 978-1-60710-075-1 / ISBN-10: 1-60710-075-4

Library of Congress Cataloging-in-Publication Data

Instant genius smart mouths.
        p. cm.
 ISBN 978-1-60710-075-1
1. Quotations, English. I. Portable Press (Ashland, Or.)
PN6081.I555 2009
082—dc22

2009023044

First Printing
1 2 3 4 5 6 7 8 9 13 12 11 10 09

ACKNOWLEDGMENTS

The editors would like to thank the people whose
advice and assistance made this book possible.

Gordon Javna · Thom Little · Jay Newman · Amy Miller
Dan Mansfield · Brian Boone · Michael Brunsfeld · Sharilyn Carroll
Melinda Allman · Eric Warren · Jeff Altemus · Christine DeGueron
Bruce Bayard · JoAnn Padgett · Lisa Meyers · Monica Maestas
Mary Skiver · Ginger Winters · Oscar Levant · Gary Bundzak
Amy Ly · Sydney Stanley · David Calder · Scarab Media
(Mr.) Mustard Press · Publishers Group West
Raincoast Books · Porter the Wonder Dog

INTRODUCTION

Nicolas de Chamfort once said, "Most anthologists of quotations are like those who eat cherries or oysters: first picking the best ones and winding up by eating everything"—and man, are we full! We've picked through tens of thousands of quotations from around the world and from thousands of years ago right up to the present to infuse *Instant Genius: Smart Mouths* with not only the best oysters and cherries, but also the best pickles, cheeses, goulashes, olives, candies, wines, and liqueurs of quotations to create a cornucopia of wisdom, weirdness, and wit.

Like the first book in our *Instant Genius* series, *Smart Mouths* is laid out in a scroll format, moving through twenty-two chapters from one topic to another in a natural, flowing manner that allows for quick but thought-provoking entertainment. Some quotes stand alone; others are grouped in categories, such as travel, genius, childhood, sanity, religion, and sex, and some less expected ones—including household appliances, submarines, junk, and worms. We did this because no matter how hard we try to shoehorn our experiences into tidy categories, life doesn't always cooperate—it's not that neat. And some observations are singular and defy conventional grouping...just as readers do.

So jump right in. Start at the beginning and read it all the way through, or just open it anywhere and see what's waiting for you—maybe you'll encounter the precise words you need to get you through the day.

—The Editors at the Knowledge Commons

*　　　*　　　*

"The greatest gift is a passion for reading. It is cheap, it consoles, it distracts, it excites, it gives you knowledge of the world and experience of a wide kind. It is a moral illumination."

—Elizabeth Hardwick

TRUE GENIUS

"When a true genius appears in the world, you may know him by this sign, that the dunces are all in confederacy against him."

—Jonathan Swift

"The true genius shudders at incompleteness—and usually prefers silence to saying something which is not everything it should be."

—Edgar Allan Poe

"Andy Warhol is the only genius with an IQ of 60."

—Gore Vidal

"Society develops wit, but contemplation alone forms genius."

—Madame de Stael

"Next to possessing genius myself would be the pleasure of living with one who possessed it."

—Elizabeth Prentiss

"Genius—the ability to produce fantastic amounts of equally fantastic bullsh*t that all makes perfect sense."

—Jason Zebehazy

"Real genius is nothing else but the supernatural virtue of humility in the domain of thought."

—Simone Weil

"I don't want to be a genius—I have enough problems just trying to be a man."

—Albert Camus

SEIZE THE DAY

"What a large volume of adventures may be grasped within this little span of life, by him who interests his heart in everything, and who, having eyes to see what time and chance are perpetually holding out to him as he journeyeth on his way, misses nothing he can fairly lay his hands on."

—Laurence Sterne

FOUR QUICK QUOTES

"Life seems but a quick succession of busy nothings."

—Jane Austen

"Wishing to be friends is quick work, but friendship is a slow-ripening fruit."

—Aristotle

"It's amazing how quickly nature consumes human places after we turn our backs on them. Life is a hungry thing."

—Scott Westerfeld

"I think a good gift for the president would be a chocolate revolver. And since he is so busy, you'd probably have to run up to him real quick and give it to him."

—Jack Handey

TO WIT

"The only reason some people get lost in thought is because it's unfamiliar territory."

—Paul Fix

"I'd love to see Christ come back to crush the spirit of hate and make men put down their guns. I'd also like just one more hit single."

—Tiny Tim

"If all the world's a stage, I want to operate the trapdoor."

—Paul Beatty

"Nostalgia is like a grammar lesson: you find the present tense, but the past perfect."

—Owens Lee Pomeroy

"There's nothing wrong with being shallow…as long as you're insightful about it."

—Dennis Miller

"Do you think that every time someone has acupuncture there's a voodoo doll out there having a really bad day?"

—Caryn Leschen

GET READY…

"There are no true beginnings but in pain. When you understand that and can withstand pain, then you're almost ready to start."

—Leslie Woolf Hedley

COME TOGETHER…

"When men dream, each has his own world. When they are awake, they have a common world."

—Heraclitus of Ephesus

"We are all in this together…by ourselves."

—Lily Tomlin

"When a hundred men stand together, each of them loses his mind and gets another one."

—Friedrich Nietzsche

"There would be no society if living together depended upon understanding each other."

—Eric Hoffer

"A human being is part of a whole, called by us the universe, a part limited in time and space. He experiences himself, his thoughts and feelings, as something separated from the rest a kind of optical delusion of his consciousness. This delusion is a kind of prison for us, restricting us to our personal desires and to affection for a few persons nearest us. Our task must be to free ourselves from this prison by widening our circles of compassion to embrace all living creatures and the whole of nature in its beauty."

—Albert Einstein

"Those who talk of unity sometimes mean a communal grave."

—Victor Shenderovich

FAMOUS FIRST WORDS

"That's one small step for man, one giant leap for mankind."

—Neil Armstrong, on the Moon

FAMOUS LAST WORDS

"That was the best ice-cream soda I ever tasted."

—Lou Costello, 1959

"I hope the exit is joyful and hope never to return."

—Frida Kahlo, 1954

"I'm bored with it all."

—Winston Churchill, 1965

"Is it not meningitis?"

—**Louisa May Alcott, 1888**

"Leave the shower curtain on the inside of the tub."

—**Conrad Hilton, 1979**

"Die? I should say not, dear fellow. No Barrymore would allow such a conventional thing to happen to him."

—**John Barrymore, 1942**

"This is absurd, this is absurd."

—**Sigmund Freud, 1939**

"Lord help my poor soul."

—**Edgar Allan Poe, 1849**

"Write...write...pencil...paper."

—**Heinrich Heine, 1856**

"Get my swan costume ready."

—**Anna Pavlova, 1931**

"Leave me alone. I'm fine."

—**Barry White, 2003**

"Is everyone else alright?"

—**Robert F. Kennedy, 1968**

CONAN THE COMEDIAN

"California governor Arnold Schwarzenegger said America needs to work together to conserve oil. Then Arnold lit a cigar and drove over the crowd in his Hummer."

—Conan O'Brien

DUCK, DUCK, GOOSE

"To listen is an effort, and just to hear is no merit. A duck hears also."

—Igor Stravinsky

"Always behave like a duck—keep calm and unruffled on the surface but paddle like the devil underneath."

—Jacob Braude

"The snow goose need not bathe to make itself white. Neither need you do anything but be yourself."

—Lao Tzu

THE HUMAN CONDITION

"Life is a tragedy for those who feel, and a comedy for those who think."

—Jean de la Bruyère

"Life is like a very short visit to a toy shop between birth and death."

—Desmond Morris

"Life is a moderately good play with a badly written third act."

—Truman Capote

"Life is like a dogsled team. If you ain't the lead dog, the scenery never changes."

—Lewis Grizzard

"Here I am trying to live, or rather, I am trying to teach the death within me how to live."

—Jean Cocteau

"Life is just one damned thing after another."

—Elbert Hubbard

SMART MOUTH: DOUGLAS ADAMS

"It is no coincidence that in no known language does the phrase 'As pretty as an airport' appear."

"It is a rare mind indeed that can render the hitherto nonexistent blindingly obvious. The cry 'I could have thought of that' is a very popular and misleading one, for the fact is that they didn't, and a very significant and revealing fact it is too."

"One always overcompensates for disabilities. I'm thinking of having my entire body surgically removed."

"There is a theory which states that if ever for any reason anyone discovers what exactly the universe is for and why it is here it will instantly disappear and be replaced by something even more bizarre and inexplicable. There is another that states that this has already happened."

"The fact that we live at the bottom of a deep gravity well, on the surface of a gas-covered planet going around a nuclear fireball 90 million miles away and think this to be normal is obviously some indication of how skewed our perspective tends to be."

THE MEANING OF DARK

"If the whole universe has no meaning, we should never have found out that it has no meaning: just as, if there were no light in the universe and therefore no creatures with eyes, we should never know it was dark. Dark would be without meaning."

—C. S. Lewis

THE CAT IN THE QUOTE

"After scolding one's cat one looks into its face and is seized by the ugly suspicion that it understood every word. And has filed it for reference."

—Charlotte Gray

"A cat sleeps fat, yet walks thin."

—Fred Schwab

"With the qualities of cleanliness, affection, patience, dignity, and courage that cats have, how many of us, I ask you, would be capable of becoming cats?"

—Fernand Mery

"Cats are notoriously sore losers. Coming in second best, especially to someone as poorly coordinated as a human being, grates their sensibility."

—Stephen Baker

"Cat people are different, to the extent that they generally are not conformists. How could they be, with a cat running their lives?"

—**Louis Camuti**

"I love cats because I enjoy my home; and little by little, they become its visible soul."

—**Jean Cocteau**

TO BE, OR...

"No one ever lacks a good reason for suicide."

—**Cesare Pavese**

"That life is worth living is the most necessary of assumptions, and, were it not assumed, the most impossible of conclusions."

—**George Santayana**

"Once I tried to kill myself with a bungee cord. I kept almost dying."

—**Steven Wright**

"When I get sick of what men do, I have only to walk a few steps in another direction to see what spiders do. Or what the weather does. This sustains me very well indeed."

—**E. B. White**

"Suicide is man's way of telling God, 'You can't fire me—I quit.'"

—**Bill Maher**

Razors pain you;
Rivers are damp;
Acids stain you;
And drugs cause cramp.
Guns aren't lawful;
Nooses give;
Gas smells awful;
You might as well live.

—Dorothy Parker, "Resume"

KNOW THYSELF

"'Know thyself?' If I knew myself I'd run away."

—Johann Wolfgang von Goethe

"Each morning when I awake, I experience again a supreme pleasure—that of being Salvador Dalí."

—Salvador Dalí

"I am the only person in the world I should like to know thoroughly."

—Oscar Wilde

"My one regret in life is that I am not someone else."

—Woody Allen

I may be smelly and I may be old,
Rough in my pebbles, reedy in my pools,
But where my fish float by I bless their swimming
And I like the people to bathe in me,
especially women.

—Stevie Smith

ON ART

"[My grandfather] collects cigarette butts, glues them together, and makes pictures of naked ladies, then sprays the whole thing silver. His stuff was taking trash and making it art. I guess I try to do that, too."

—**Beck**

"If I could tell you what it meant, there would be no point in dancing it."

—**Isadora Duncan**

"Irresponsibility is part of the pleasure of all art; it is the part the schools cannot recognize."

—**James Joyce**

"Without art, the crudeness of reality would make the world unbearable."

—**George Bernard Shaw**

"Art, like morality, consists of drawing the line somewhere."

—**G. K. Chesterton**

"Art is a lie that makes us realize the truth."

—**Pablo Picasso**

THE MEANING OF LIFE

"But now I have come to believe that the whole world is an enigma, a harmless enigma that is made terrible by our own mad attempt to interpret it as though it had an underlying truth."

—**Umberto Eco**

"The fact that life has no meaning is a reason to live—moreover, the only one."

—E. M. Cioran

"My life has no purpose, no direction, no aim, no meaning, and yet I'm happy. I can't figure it out. What am I doing right?"

—Charles Schulz

"Living apart and at peace with myself, I came to realize more vividly the meaning of the doctrine of acceptance. To refrain from giving advice, to refrain from meddling in the affairs of others, to refrain, even though the motives be the highest, from tampering with another's way of life—so simple, yet so difficult for an active spirit. Hands off!"

—Henry Miller

"Through faith man experiences the meaning of the world; through action he is to give to it meaning."

—Leo Braeck

ST. PETER?

"When did I realize I was God? Well, I was praying and I suddenly realized I was talking to myself."

—Peter O'Toole

SMART MOUTH: OSCAR LEVANT

"The first thing I do in the morning is brush my teeth and sharpen my tongue."

"Underneath this flabby exterior is an enormous lack of character."

"I envy people who drink. At least they have something to blame everything on."

"I'm going to memorize your name and throw my head away."

"Strip away the phony tinsel of Hollywood and you'll find the real tinsel underneath."

"Happiness isn't something you experience; it's something you remember."

"I'm a concert pianist. That's a pretentious way of saying I'm unemployed at the moment."

"Every time I look at you I get a fierce desire to be lonesome."

HMMM...

"Nansen saw the monks of the eastern and western halls fighting over a cat. He seized the cat and told the monks: 'If any of you say a good word, you can save the cat.' No one answered. So Nansen boldly cut the cat in two pieces. That evening Joshu returned and Nansen told him about this. Joshu removed his sandals and, placing them on his head, walked out. Nansen said: 'If you had been there, you could have saved the cat.'"

—**Zen koan**

LET'S DANCE

"He who cannot dance will say: 'The drum is bad.'"

—**Ashanti (Ghana) proverb**

"To me, boxing is like a ballet, except there's no music, no choreography, and the dancers hit each other."

—**Jack Handey**

"Ballet: Men wearing pants so tight that you can tell what religion they are."

—Robin Williams

"Never give a sword to a man who can't dance."

—Confucius

SOLITAIRE

"The only real progress lies in learning to be wrong all alone."

—Albert Camus

MAN AND THE ANIMALS

"Drinking without being thirsty and making love at any time, Madame, are the only things that distinguish us from other animals."

—Beaumarchais

"I have been studying the traits and dispositions of the 'lower animals' (so called) and contrasting them with the traits and dispositions of man. I find the result humiliating to me."

—Mark Twain

"Life is as dear to a mute creature as it is to man. Just as one wants happiness and fears pain, just as one wants to live and not die, so do other creatures."

—Dalai Lama

"Man is the only animal that can remain on friendly terms with the victim he intends to eat until he eats them."

—Samuel Butler

The prince ordered a solemn reception,
offered wine to the seabird
in the Sacred precinct,
called for musicians to play
the compositions of Shun,
slaughtered cattle to nourish it.
Dazed with symphonies,
the unhappy seabird died of despair.

—Thomas Merton

"If a group of beings from another planet were to land on Earth—beings who considered themselves as superior to you as you feel yourself to be to other animals—would you concede them the rights over you that you assume over other animals?"

—George Bernard Shaw

"Weaseling out of things is good. It's what separates us from the other animals...except the weasel."

—Homer Simpson

STYLE GENIUS

"Long hair minimizes the need for barbers; socks can be done without; one leather jacket solves the coat problem for many years; suspenders are superfluous."

—Albert Einstein

CHAPTER 2

IMPOSSIBLE THINGS

"Alice laughed. 'There's no use trying,' she said. 'One can't believe impossible things.' 'I dare say you haven't had much practice,' said the Queen. 'When I was your age, I always did it for half an hour a day. Why, sometimes I've believed as many as six impossible things before breakfast."

—Lewis Carroll, *Through the Looking-Glass*

SEX AND THE WITTY

"My girlfriend always laughs during sex—no matter what she's reading."

—Steve Jobs

"If you use the electric vibrator near water, you will come and go at the same time."

—Louise Sammons

"Seems to me the basic conflict between men and women, sexually, is that men are like firemen. To men, sex is an emergency, and no matter what we're doing we can be ready in two minutes. Women, on the other hand, are like fire. They're very exciting, but the conditions have to be exactly right for it to occur."

—Jerry Seinfeld

"When the authorities warn you of the dangers of having sex, there is an important lesson to be learned. Do not have sex with the authorities."

—Matt Groening

"We all worry about the population explosion…but we don't worry about it at the right time."

—Arthur Hoppe

"Conservatives say teaching sex education in the public schools will promote promiscuity. With our education system? If we promote promiscuity the same way we promote math or science, they've got nothing to worry about."

—Beverly Mickins

"Sexual intercourse is kicking death in the ass while singing."

—Charles Bukowski

"Why should we take sex advice from the pope? If he knows anything about it, he shouldn't."

—George Bernard Shaw

"We have reason to believe that man first walked upright to free his hands for masturbation."

—**Lily Tomlin**

"Sex—the poor man's polo."

—**Clifford Odets**

ME?

"If you're playing a poker game and you look around the table and can't tell who the sucker is, it's you."

—**Paul Newman**

WHAT IS IT GOOD FOR?

"The bomb that fell on Hiroshima fell on America too. It fell on no city, no munition plants, no docks. It erased no church, vaporized no public buildings, reduced no man to his atomic elements. But it fell, it fell."

—**Hermann Hagedorn**

"In time of war the loudest patriots are the greatest profiteers."

—**August Bebel**

"A visitor from Mars could easily pick out the civilized nations. They have the best implements of war."

—**Herbert V. Prochnow**

"War is a cowardly escape from the problems of peace."

—**Thomas Mann**

"You're an old-timer if you can remember when setting the world on fire was a figure of speech."

—Franklin P. Jones

"I believe in compulsory cannibalism. If people were forced to eat what they kill, there would be no more war."

—Abbie Hoffman

HMMM...

We milk the cow of the world, and as we do
We whisper in her ear, "You are not here."

—Richard Wilbur

SMART MOUTH: ALBERT EINSTEIN

"The most beautiful thing we can experience is the mysterious. It is the source of all true art and science. He to whom this emotion is a stranger, who no longer pauses to wonder and stand in rapt awe, is as good as dead."

"Egoism and competition are, alas, stronger forces than public spirit and sense of duty."

"A hundred times every day I remind myself that my inner and outer life depend upon the labors of other men, living and dead, and that I must exert myself in order to give in the measure I have received."

"To punish me for my contempt for authority, fate made me an authority myself."

"It would be possible to describe everything scientifically, but it would make no sense; it would be without meaning, as if you described a Beethoven symphony as a variation of wave pressure."

"The gift of fantasy has meant more to me than my talent for absorbing knowledge."

"He who joyfully marches in rank and file has already earned my contempt. He has been given a large brain by mistake, since for him the spinal cord would suffice."

"There are two ways to live your life. One is as though nothing is a miracle. The other is as though everything is."

GOT A LIGHT?

"You know it's not a good wax museum when there are wicks sticking out of people's heads."

—Stephanie Huddleson

SLAP SHOTS

"Hockey captures the essence of Canadian experience in the New World. In a land so inescapably and inhospitably cold, hockey is the chance of life, and an affirmation that despite the deathly chill of winter we are alive."

—Stephen Leacock

"Call them pros, call them mercenaries—but in fact they are just grown-up kids who have learned on the frozen creek or flooded corner lot that hockey is the greatest thrill of all."

—Lester Patrick

"We take the shortest route to the puck and arrive in ill humor."

—Bobby Clarke

"All hockey players are bilingual. They know English and profanity."

—Gordie Howe

"A good hockey player plays where the puck is. A great hockey player plays where the puck is going to be."

—Wayne Gretzky

"Some guys play hockey. Gretzky plays 40-mph chess."

—Lowell Cohn

"My other car is a Zamboni."

—bumper sticker

KURTOPIA

"Human beings will be happier—not when they cure cancer or get to Mars or eliminate racial prejudice or flush Lake Erie—but when they find ways to inhabit primitive communities again. That's my utopia."

—Kurt Vonnegut

ON FOREIGN LANDS

"I've always wanted to go to Switzerland to see what the army does with those wee red knives."

—Billy Connolly

"New Zealand is a country of thirty thousand million sheep, three million of whom think they are human."

—Dame Edna (Barry Humphries)

"Poor Mexico, so far from God and so close to the United States."

—Porfirio Diaz

"Homosexuality in Russia is a crime and the punishment is seven years in prison, locked up with the other men. There is a three-year waiting list."

—Yakov Smirnoff

"South Africa, renowned both far and wide
For politics and little else besides."

—Roy Dunnachie Campbell

"The only nation I've ever been tempted to feel really racist about are the Swiss—a whole country of phobic hand washers living in a giant Barclays Bank."

—Jonathan Raban

"India was the mother of our race and Sanskrit the mother of Europe's languages. She was the mother of our philosophy, mother through the Arabs, of much of our mathematics, mother through Buddha, of the ideals embodied in Christianity, mother through village communities of self-government and democracy. Mother India is in many ways the mother of us all."

—Will Durant

"Italy is a paradise for horses and hell for women."

—German proverb

"Canada is the essence of not being. Not English, not American, it is the mathematic of not being. And a subtle flavor—we're more like celery as a flavor."

—Mike Myers

"Every country gets the circus it deserves. Spain gets bullfights. Italy gets the Catholic Church. America gets Hollywood."

—Erica Jong

BECK AND CALL

"I always try to leave in the mistakes—that's the interesting stuff. If someone walked into the room while you were doing a little falsetto lead and said, 'The burritos are here,' that's the best part. That's the part people will remember."

—Beck

WORDS ON BOOKS

"We need books that affect us like a disaster. That grieve us deeply. Like the death of someone we loved more than ourselves. Like being banished into the forests far from everyone. Like a suicide. A book must be the ax for the frozen sea inside us."

—Franz Kafka

"Never judge a book by its movie."

—J. W. Eagan

You may have tangible wealth untold;
Caskets of jewels and coffers of gold.
Richer than I you can never be—
I had a mother who read to me.

—Strickland Gillilan

"A library is a hospital for the mind."

—Anonymous

The body of Benjamin Franklin,
Printer,
Like the covering
Of an old book
Its contents torn out
And stript of its lettering
And gilding
Lies here, food for worms;
But the work
Shall not be lost,
It will (as he believed)
Appear once more,
In a new
And more beautiful edition,
Corrected and amended
By the author.

**—Mock epitaph written
for Benjamin Franklin
by himself, 1728**

"It often requires more courage to read some books than it does
to fight a battle."

—Sutton Elbert Griggs

"A book is a version of the world. If you do not like it, ignore it; or offer your own version in return."

—Salman Rushdie

"Even bad books are books, and therefore sacred."

—Günter Grass

"Every night, I have to read a book, so that my mind will stop thinking about things that I stress about."

—Britney Spears

DON'T FORGET THE SIXTIES

"The thing the Sixties did was to show us the possibilities and the responsibility that we all had. It wasn't the answer. It just gave us a glimpse of the possibility."

—John Lennon

"On one level the Sixties revolt was an impressive illustration of Lenin's remark that the capitalist will sell you the rope to hang him with."

—Ellen Willis

"The Sixties were when hallucinogenic drugs were really, really big. And I don't think it's a coincidence that we had the type of shows we had then, like *The Flying Nun*."

—Ellen DeGeneres

"The freedom that women were supposed to have found in the Sixties largely boiled down to easy contraception and abortion; things to make life easier for men, in fact."

—Julie Burchill

"The Sixties were an oyster decade: slippery, luxurious, and reportedly aphrodisiac they slipped down the historical throat without touching the sides."

—Julian Barnes

"I like to think of my behavior in the Sixties as a 'learning experience.' Then again, I like to think of anything stupid I've done as a 'learning experience.' It makes me feel less stupid."

—P. J. O'Rourke

WRITERS ON DRINKING

"Always do sober what you said you'd do drunk. That will teach you to keep your mouth shut."

—Ernest Hemingway

"The harsh, useful things of the world, from pulling teeth to digging potatoes, are best done by men who are as starkly sober as so many convicts in the death-house, but the lovely and useless things, the charming and exhilarating things, are best done by men with, as the phrase is, a few sheets in the wind."

—H. L. Mencken

"He drank not as an epicure, but barbarously, with a speed and dispatch, as if he were performing a homicidal function, as if he had to kill something inside himself; a worm that would not die."

—Charles Baudelaire, on Edgar Allan Poe

"Unlike some men, I had never drunk for boldness or charm or wit; I had used alcohol for precisely what it was, a depressant to check the mental exhilaration produced by extended sobriety."

—Frederick Exley

"I have the feeling that drinking is a form of suicide where you're allowed to return to life and begin all over the next day. It's like killing yourself, and then you're reborn. I guess I've lived about ten or fifteen thousand lives now."

—Charles Bukowski

A DEEP THOUGHT

"Language furnishes the best proof that a law accepted by a community is a thing that is tolerated and not a rule to which all freely consent."

—Ferdinand De Saussure

A DEEPER THOUGHT

"He who seeks vengeance must dig two graves: one for his enemy and one for himself."

—Chinese proverb

WHEN IN DOUBT...

"Our doubts are traitors, and make us lose the good we oft might win by fearing to attempt."

—William Shakespeare

"I slept with faith and found a corpse in my arms on awakening; I drank and danced all night with doubt and found her a virgin in the morning."

—Aleister Crowley

"To doubt is worse than to have lost; and to despair is but to antedate those miseries that must fall on us."

—Philip Massinger

"Doubt is uncomfortable, certainty is ridiculous."

—Voltaire

You can doubt anything
If you think about it long enough
Cuz what happened always adjusts to fit
What happened after that.

—Ani Difranco

"When in doubt, make a fool of yourself. There is a microscopically thin line between being brilliantly creative and acting like the most gigantic idiot on earth. So what the hell, leap."

—Cynthia Heimel

"The only thing that makes life possible is permanent, intolerable uncertainty; not knowing what comes next."

—Ursula K. LeGuin

"Isn't it the moment of most profound doubt that gives birth to new certainties? Perhaps hopelessness is the very soil that nourishes human hope; perhaps one could never find sense in life without first experiencing its absurdity."

—Vaclav Havel

There lives more faith in honest doubt
Believe me, than in half the creeds.

—Alfred, Lord Tennyson

"Great doubts...deep wisdom. Small doubts...little wisdom."

—Chinese proverb

"If you would be a real seeker after truth, it is necessary that at least once in your life you doubt, as far as possible, all things."

— **René Descartes**

PIGARO?

"Never try to teach a pig to sing. It wastes your time and annoys the pig."

—**Author unknown**

THREE FOR SEEING

"Stop a moment, cease your work, and look around you."

—**Thomas Carlyle**

"The real voyage of discovery consists of not in seeking new landscapes but in having new eyes."

—**Marcel Proust**

"The greatest thing a human being ever does is to see something and tell what he sees in a plain way."

—**John Ruskin**

ON FOOD

"A gourmet who thinks of calories is like a tart who looks at her watch."

—**James Beard**

"There is a lot more juice in grapefruit than meets the eye."

—**Anonymous**

"I went into a McDonald's yesterday and said, 'I'd like some fries.' The girl at the counter said, 'Would you like some fries with that?'"

—Jay Leno

"Fish, to taste right, must swim three times—in water, in butter, and in wine."

—Polish proverb

"Watermelon—it's a good fruit. You eat, you drink, you wash your face."

—Enrico Caruso

"You can never have enough garlic. With enough garlic, you can eat the *New York Times*."

—Morley Safer

"'When you wake up in the morning, Pooh,' said Piglet at last, 'what's the first thing you say to yourself?' 'What's for breakfast?' said Pooh. 'What do you say, Piglet?' 'I say, I wonder what's going to happen exciting today?' said Piglet. Pooh nodded thoughtfully. 'It's the same thing,' he said."

—A. A. Milne

"You know an odd feeling? Sitting on the toilet eating a chocolate candy bar."

—George Carlin

HMMM...

"A Taoist master was sitting naked in his mountain cabin, meditating. A group of Confucianists entered the door of his hut, having hiked up the mountain intending to lecture him on the rules of proper conduct. When they saw the sage sitting naked before them, they were shocked and asked, 'What are you doing, sitting in your hut without any pants on?' The sage replied, 'This entire universe is my hut. This little hut is my pants. What are you fellows doing inside my pants?'"

—James N. Powell

AMORE

"Love isn't finding a perfect person. It's seeing an imperfect person perfectly."

—Sam Keen

"Love is like the measles. The older you get it, the worse the attack."

—Mary Roberts Rinehart

"To love deeply in one direction makes us more loving in all others."

—Anne-Sophie Swetchine

"Maybe love is like luck. You have to go all the way to find it."

—Robert Mitchum

"Passion makes the world go round. Love just makes it a safer place."

—Ice-T

"Love is the difficult realization that something other than oneself is real."

—Iris Murdoch

"Love is being stupid together."

—Paul Valery

"Love is an exploding cigar we willingly smoke."

—Lynda Barry

"Love is a snowmobile racing across the tundra, and then suddenly it flips over, pinning you underneath. At night, the ice weasels come."

—Matt Groening

LET'S TALK

"Conversation should be pleasant without scurrility, witty without affectation, free without indecency, learned without conceitedness, novel without falsehood."

—William Shakespeare

"Conversation is like playing tennis with a ball made of Krazy Putty that keeps coming back over the net in a different shape."

—David John Lodge

"It was impossible to get a conversation going; everybody was talking too much."

—Yogi Berra

"Conversation between Adam and Eve must have been difficult at times because they had nobody to talk about."

—Agnes Repplier

"Anyone who thinks the art of conversation is dead ought to tell a child to go to bed."

—Robert C. Gallagher

"A sudden silence in the middle of a conversation suddenly brings us back to essentials: it reveals how dearly we must pay for the invention of speech."

—E. M. Cioran

NO SHORTCUTS

"There is no shortcut to art, one has to work hard, be open and flexible in your mind, keep the child alive inside you, and through a whole lifetime be ready to learn new things and—of course—be mentally prepared for a hard punch on your nose, especially when you think you are doing well."

—Bente Borsum

SMART MOUTH: ANONYMOUS

"A flashlight is a case for holding dead batteries."

"I'm a Marxist—of the Groucho variety."

"Time is that quality of nature which keeps events from happening all at once. Lately it doesn't seem to be working."

"The nice thing about standards is, there are so many to choose from."

"Nine out of ten people who change their minds are wrong the second time too."

"A professor is one who talks in someone else's sleep."

"Don't let yourself forget what it's like to be sixteen."

"The philosophy exam was a piece of cake—which was a bit of a surprise, actually, because I was expecting some questions on a sheet of paper."

"Going to church doesn't make you a Christian any more than standing in a garage makes you a car."

"A closed mouth gathers no feet."

"A metaphor is like a simile."

"Mary had a little lamb. And the doctor fainted."

"Nobody knows the age of the human race, but everybody agrees that it is old enough to know better."

CHAPTER 3

A GOAT FROM A WOOLF

"If we didn't live adventurously, plucking the wild goat by
the beard, and trembling over precipices, we should never be
depressed, I've no doubt; but already should be faded, fatalistic
and aged."

—Virginia Woolf

FROM THE LABORATORY

"Should we force science down the throats of those that have
no taste for it? Is it our duty to drag them kicking and screaming
into the twenty-first century? I am afraid that it is."

—George Porter

"Science is a first-rate piece of furniture for a man's upper chamber, if he has common sense on the ground floor."

—Oliver Wendell Holmes Sr.

"Science is not a sacred cow. Science is a horse. Don't worship it. Feed it."

—Abba Eban

"The most exciting phrase to hear in science, the one that heralds new discoveries, is not 'Eureka!' but 'Hmmm, that's funny...'"

—Isaac Asimov

"Research is what I'm doing when I don't know what I'm doing."

—Wernher von Braun

"The microwave oven is the consolation prize in our struggle to understand physics."

—Jason Love

"Physics isn't a religion. If it were, we'd have a much easier time raising money."

—Leon Lederman

"Not only is the universe stranger than we think, it is stranger than we *can* think."

—Werner Heisenberg

"Physics is like sex: sure, it may give some practical results, but that's not why we do it."

—**Richard Feynman**

SMART MOUTH?

"Marge, promise me you'll put me in a home. It's like being a baby, only you're old enough to appreciate it."

—**Homer Simpson**

AS LUCK WOULD HAVE IT...

"I believe in luck: how else can you explain the success of those you dislike?"

—**Jean Cocteau**

"Depend on the rabbit's foot if you will, but remember it didn't work for the rabbit."

—**R. E. Shay**

"Luck never gives; it only lends."

—**Swedish proverb**

> Luck is not chance—
> It's Toil—
> Fortune's expensive smile
> Is earned—
> The Father of the Mine
> Is that old-fashioned Coin
> We spurned—

—**Emily Dickinson**

"With a little luck, many martyrs would have become executioners."

—**Roberto Gervaso**

"If a man who cannot count finds a four-leaf clover, is he lucky?"

—**Stanislaw J. Lec**

"It's bad luck to be superstitious."

—**Andrew W. Mathis**

A WORD TO THE WISE

"Touch not the flute when drums are sounding around; when fools have the word, the wise will be silent."

—**Johann Gottfried von Herder**

YOU ARE FAMILY

"Blood is thicker than water."

—**Anonymous**

"There's an awful lot of blood around that water is thicker than."

—**Mignon McLaughlin**

"There is no such thing as 'fun for the whole family.'"

—**Jerry Seinfeld**

"Having a family is like having a bowling alley installed in your brain."

—**Martin Mull**

"The family. We were a strange little band of characters trudging through life sharing diseases and toothpaste, coveting one another's desserts, hiding shampoo, borrowing money, locking each other out of our rooms, inflicting pain and kissing to heal it in the same instant, loving, laughing, defending, and trying to figure out the common thread that bound us all together."

—Erma Bombeck

"If you have an enormous nose, I suppose you can have an operation to make it smaller, but you can't operate away an undesirable family member."

—John Simon

"If you ever start feeling like you have the goofiest, craziest, most dysfunctional family in the world, all you have to do is go to a state fair. Because five minutes at the fair, you'll be going, 'You know, we're alright. We are dang near royalty.'"

—Jeff Foxworthy

"The family—that dear octopus from whose tentacles we never quite escape nor, in our innermost hearts, ever quite wish to."

—Dodie Smith

"Other things may change us, but we start and end with family."

—Anthony Brandt

HMMM...

"Is man one of God's blunders, or is God one of man's blunders?"

—Friedrich Nietzsche

WISDOM FROM JAVA

"I believe humans get a lot done, not because we're smart, but because we have thumbs so we can make coffee."

—Flash Rosenberg

"I've taken up meditation. I like to have an espresso first to make it more challenging."

—Betsy Salkind

"The voodoo priest and all his powders were as nothing compared to espresso, cappuccino, and mocha, which are stronger than all the religions of the world combined, and perhaps stronger than the human soul itself."

—Mark Helprin

"I think if I were a woman I'd wear coffee as a perfume."

—John Van Druten

"A morning without coffee is like sleep."

—Anonymous

FOUR KINGS

"I refuse to accept the view that mankind is so tragically bound to the starless midnight of racism and war that the bright daybreak of peace and brotherhood can never become reality. I believe that unarmed truth and unconditional love will have the final word in reality. That is why right, temporarily defeated, is stronger than evil triumphant."

—Martin Luther King Jr.

"Martin Luther King took us to the mountaintop; I want to take us to the bank."

—Don King

"I've said that playing the blues is like having to be black twice. Stevie Ray Vaughan missed on both counts, but I never noticed."

—B. B. King

"He had a massive stroke. He died with his tie on. Do you think that could be our generation's equivalent of that old saying about dying with your boots on?"

—Stephen King

GOOD ADVICE

"Before you judge a man, walk a mile in his shoes. After that, who cares? He's a mile away and you've got his shoes."

—Billy Connolly

THREE RULES TO GRIPE BY

"The longer one saves something before throwing it away, the sooner it will be needed after it is thrown away."

—James J. Caufield

"Whenever A annoys or injures B on the pretense of saving or improving X, A is a scoundrel."

—H. L. Mencken

"Misquotations are the only quotations that are never misquoted."

—Hesketh Pearson

WATCH YOUR STEP

"The adjective is the banana peel of the parts of speech."

—Clifton Fadiman

ON AMERICA

"Europe was created by history. America was created by philosophy."

—Margaret Thatcher

"America is a country that doesn't know where it is going but is determined to set a speed record getting there."

—Laurence J. Peter

"America is a large, friendly dog in a very small room. Every time it wags its tail, it knocks over a chair."

—Arnold Toynbee

"America is a vast conspiracy to make you happy."

—John Updike

"America did not invent human rights. In a very real sense, it is the other way round. Human rights invented America."

—Jimmy Carter

"There are two Americas. One is the America of Lincoln and Adlai Stevenson; the other is the America of Teddy Roosevelt and the modern superpatriots. One is generous and humane, the other narrowly egotistical; one is self-critical, the other self-righteous; one is sensible, the other romantic; one is good-humored, the other solemn; one is inquiring, the other pontificating; one is moderate, the other filled with passionate intensity; one is judicious and the other arrogant in the use of great power."

—J. William Fulbright

"There's a phrase we live by in America: 'In God We Trust.' It's right there where Jesus would want it: on our money."

—Stephen Colbert

PET FACE BOYS?

"Guys are lucky because they get to grow mustaches. I wish I could. It's like having a little pet for your face."

—Anita Wise

SMART MOUTH: STEPHEN HAWKING

"We are just an advanced breed of monkeys on a minor planet of a very average star. But we can understand the universe. That makes us something very special."

"I think computer viruses should count as life. I think it says something about human nature that the only form of life we have created so far is purely destructive. We've created life in our own image."

"Why is the universe as we observe it? The answer, of course, is that if it were otherwise, there would not be anyone to ask the question."

"As we shall see, the concept of time has no meaning before the beginning of the universe. This was first pointed out by St. Augustine. When asked: What did God do before he created the universe? Augustine didn't reply: He was preparing Hell for people who asked such questions. Instead, he said that time was a property of the universe that God created, and that time did not exist before the beginning of the universe."

THAT'S THE LAW

"The law was made for one thing alone—for the exploitation of those who don't understand it."

—Bertolt Brecht

WE ADVISE YOU TO...

"Become who you are."

—Friedrich Nietzsche

"Stay busy, get plenty of exercise, and don't drink too much. Then again, don't drink too little."

—Herman "Jackrabbit" Smith-Johannsen

"The words 'I am...' are potent words; be careful what you hitch them to. The thing you're claiming has a way of reaching back and claiming you."

—A. L. Kitselman

"Be sure to wear a good cologne, a nice aftershave lotion, and a strong underarm deodorant. And it might be a good idea to wear some clothes, too."

—George Burns

"I would advise you to keep your overhead down; avoid a major drug habit; play everyday, and take it in front of other people. They need to hear it, and you need them to hear it."

—James Taylor

"Beware of advice, even this."

—Carl Sandburg

GOOD MEDICINE

"I observe the physician with the same diligence as the disease."

—John Donne

"If you are too smart to pay the doctor, you had better be too smart to get ill."

—African proverb

"The art of medicine consists in amusing the patient while nature cures the disease."

—Voltaire

"Our profession is the only one which works unceasingly to annihilate itself."

—Dr. Martin H. Fischer

"There are more old drunkards than old physicians."

—François Rabelais

"Never go to a doctor whose office plants have died."

—Erma Bombeck

FOUR-LETTER WORK

"My father taught me to work; he did not teach me to love it. I never did like to work, and I don't deny it. I'd rather read, tell stories, crack jokes, talk, laugh—anything but work."

—Abraham Lincoln

"Opportunity is missed by most because it is dressed in overalls and looks like work."

—Thomas Edison

"I do not like work even when someone else does it."

—Mark Twain

"By working faithfully eight hours a day, you may eventually get to be a boss and work twelve hours a day."

—Robert Frost

"Hard work never killed anybody, but why take a chance?"

—Edgar Bergen

"Anyone can do any amount of work provided it isn't the work he is supposed to be doing at that moment."

—Robert Benchley

"It wasn't raining when Noah built the ark."

—Howard Ruff

TWO DICKS

"Finishing second in the Olympics gets you silver. Finishing second in politics gets you oblivion."

—Richard M. Nixon

"Principle is okay up to a certain point, but principle doesn't do any good if you lose."

—Dick Cheney

THE BEST DAMN QUOTES
IN THE HISTORY OF THE UNIVERSE

"Exaggeration is a truth that has lost its temper."

—Kahlil Gibran

"Exaggeration is a blood relation to falsehood and nearly as blamable."

—Hosea Ballou

"Exaggeration, the inseparable companion of greatness."

—Voltaire

"By speaking, by thinking, we undertake to clarify things, and that forces us to exacerbate them, dislocate them, schematize them. Every concept is in itself an exaggeration."

—José Ortega y Gasset

"If you add to the truth, you subtract from it."

—The Talmud

"There are people so addicted to exaggeration they can't tell the truth without lying."

—Josh Billings

BOO?

"Considering how dangerous everything is, nothing is really very frightening."

—Gertrude Stein

SMART MOUTH: MARK TWAIN

"I thoroughly disapprove of duels. If a man should challenge me, I would take him kindly and forgivingly by the hand and lead him to a quiet place and kill him."

"Adam was the only man who, when he said a good thing, knew that nobody said it before him."

"The fact that man knows right from wrong proves his intellectual superiority to the other creatures; but the fact that he can do wrong proves his moral inferiority to any creature that cannot."

"Reader, suppose you were an idiot. And suppose you were a member of Congress. But I repeat myself..."

"Whenever the literary German dives into a sentence, that is the last you are going to see of him till he emerges on the other side of his Atlantic with his verb in his mouth."

"I have no special regard for Satan; but, I can at least claim that I have no prejudice against him. It may even be that I lean a little his way, on account of his not having a fair show. All religions issue bibles against him, and say the most injurious things about him, but we never hear his side. We have none but the evidence for the prosecution, and yet we have rendered the verdict. To my mind, this is irregular. It is un-English, it is un-American; it is French."

"I can teach anybody how to get what they want out of life. The problem is that I can't find anybody who can tell me what they want."

ON HISTORY

"History would be a wonderful thing—if it were only true."

—Leo Tolstoy

"History is the present. That's why every generation writes it anew. But what most people think of as history is its end product, myth."

—E. L. Doctorow

"History is, in part, a series of madmen deluding people into parting with their children for loathsome and tragic schemes."

—Sting

"History is simply a piece of paper covered with print; the main thing is still to make history, not to write it."

—Otto von Bismarck

"In times like these, it's helpful to remember that there have always been times like these."
—Paul Harvey

LOOKING FORWARD

"Trying to predict the future is like trying to drive down a country road at night with no lights while looking out the back window."
—Peter F. Drucker

"When it comes to the future, there are three kinds of people: those who let it happen, those who make it happen, and those who wonder what happened."
—John M. Richardson Jr.

"Successful people seek out their futures from the present; failures seek out their futures from the past."
—Li Ao

Drink and dance and laugh and lie,
Love, the reeling midnight through,
For tomorrow we shall die!
(But, alas, we never do.)
—Dorothy Parker

"The distance from here to a brighter future can only be measured in light-years."
—Rasto Zakic

"The future is here. It's just not widely distributed yet."
—William Gibson

"The future is not a result of choices among alternative paths offered by the present, but a place that is created—created first in the mind and will, created next in activity. The future is not some place we are going to, but one we are creating. The paths are not to be found, but made, and the activity of making them, changes both the maker and the destination."

—Deborah James

DEADLY WEAPUNS

"The goodness of the true pun is in the direct ratio of its intolerability."

—Edgar Allan Poe

"You can't make a *Hamlet* without breaking a few egos."

—William Goldman

"A pun is the lowest form of humor, unless you thought of it yourself."

—Doug Larson

"*Carpe per diem*: seize the check."

—Robin Williams

"Puns are little 'plays on words' that a certain breed of person loves to spring on you and then look at you in a certain self-satisfied way to indicate that he thinks that you must think that he is by far the cleverest person on Earth now that Benjamin Franklin is dead, when in fact what you are thinking is that if this person ever ends up in a lifeboat, the other passengers will hurl him overboard by the end of the first day even if they have plenty of food and water."

—Dave Barry

"I've always relished wordplay and have a consuming interest in culinary puns. Sometimes I'll loaf around all day, devising bone mots just for the halibut."

—Mark Morton

"I'm an incorrigible punster. Do not incorrige me."

—Anonymous

SMART MOUTH: AMELIA EARHART

"Better do a good deed near at home than go far away to burn incense."

"The stars seemed near enough to touch and never before have I seen so many. I always believed the lure of flying is the lure of beauty, but I was sure of it that night."

"The most effective way to do it is to do it."

"I want to do it because I want to do it."

"The more one does and sees and feels, the more one is able to do, and the more genuine may be one's appreciation of fundamental things like home, and love, and understanding companionship."

"There are two kinds of stones, as everyone knows, one of which rolls."

"Of course I realized there was a measure of danger. Obviously I faced the possibility of not returning when I first considered going. Once faced and settled there really wasn't any good reason to refer to it again."

CHAPTER 4

GET A GRIPE

"It's my belief we developed language because of our deep inner need to complain."

—Lily Tomlin

CALIFORNIA

"There is science, logic, reason; there is thought verified by experience. And then there is California."

—Edward Abbey

"California is a fine place to live—if you happen to be an orange."

—Fred Allen

"Los Angeles is the only town in the world where y
up in the morning and listen to the birds coughing

"California is like an artificial limb the rest of the country doesn't really need."

—Saul Bellow

"There are two million interesting people in New York—and only seventy-eight in Los Angeles."

—Neil Simon

"When an Okie moves to California, he raises the IQ of both states."

—Will Rogers

AU CONTRAIRE!

"There is the fear, common to all English-only speakers, that the chief purpose of foreign languages is to make fun of us. Otherwise, you know, why not just come out and say it?"

—Barbara Ehrenreich

HEADS UP

"If you aren't in over your head, how do you know how tall you are?"

—T. S. Eliot

"It's hard to fight an enemy who has outposts in your head."

—Sally Kempton

"If I feel physically as if the top of my head were taken off, I know that is poetry."

—Emily Dickinson

"The truth is that balding African-American men look cool when they shave their heads, whereas balding white men look like giant thumbs."

—Dave Barry

"No matter where you go or what you do, you live your entire life within the confines of your head."

—Terry Josephson

CHAIN, CHAIN, CHAIN...

"When two people are under the influence of the most violent, most insane, most delusive, and most transient of passions, they are required to swear that they will remain in that excited, abnormal, and exhausting condition until death do them part."

—George Bernard Shaw

"The best way to remember your wife's birthday is to forget it once."

—E. Joseph Cossman

"Marriage, like a submarine, is only safe if you get all the way inside."

—Frank Pittman

"I don't know. She's got gaps. I got gaps. Together we fill gaps."

—Rocky Balboa (Sylvester Stallone), *Rocky* (1976)

"You may marry the man of your dreams, ladies, but fourteen years later you're married to a couch that burps."

—Roseanne Barr

"What counts in making a happy marriage is not so much how compatible you are, but how you deal with incompatibility."

—Leo Tolstoy

"I think a man can have two, maybe three affairs, while he is married. But three is the absolute maximum. After that, you're cheating."

—Yves Montand

"A husband is what's left over once the nerve has been extracted."

—Helen Rowland

CHEERS?

"If you are young and you drink a great deal it will spoil your health, slow your mind, make you fat—in other words, turn you into an adult."

—P. J. O'Rourke

NATURE AND ART

"God manifests himself to us in the first degree through the life of the universe, and in the second degree through the thought of man. The second manifestation is not less holy than the first. The first is named Nature, the second is named Art."

—Victor Hugo

NUDISMS

"My advice to those who think they have to take off their clothes to be a star is, once you're boned, what's left to create the illusion? Let 'em wonder. I never believed in giving them too much of me."

—Mae West

"I wouldn't do nudity in films. To act with my clothes on is a performance. To act with my clothes off is a documentary."

—Julia Roberts

"I think onstage nudity is disgusting, shameful and damaging to all things American. But if I were twenty-two with a great body, it would be artistic, tasteful, patriotic, and a progressive religious experience."

—Shelley Winters

"In the nude, all that is not beautiful is obscene."

—Robert Bresson

"Someday people will grow up and realize that the only thing vile about human bodies is the small minds some people have developed within them."

—Dick Hein

"I couldn't tell if the streaker was a man or a woman because it had a bag on its head."

—Yogi Berra

"You know, it's just like being a peddler. You want two breasts? Well, here you are—two breasts. We must see to it that the man looking at the picture has at hand everything he needs to paint a nude. If you really give him everything he needs—and the best—he'll put everything where it belongs, with his own eyes. Each person will make for himself the kind of nude he wants, with the nude that I will have made for him."

—Pablo Picasso

START WORRYING

"Every time I hear the oil companies talk about solar energy I worry they've developed a plan to block out the sun."

—Will Durst

SMART MOUTH: GRACIE ALLEN

"When I was born I was so surprised I didn't talk for a year and a half."

"Smartness runs in my family. When I went to school I was so smart my teacher was in my class for five years."

"When my mother had to get dinner for eight, she'd just make enough for sixteen and only serve half."

"I often put boiling water in the freezer. Then whenever I need boiling water, I simply defrost it."

"They laughed at Joan of Arc, but she went right ahead and built it!"

"On the plus side, death is one of the few things that can be done just as easily lying down."

THE SECRET

"Here is the secret of inspiration: Tell yourself that thousands and tens of thousands of people, not very intelligent and certainly no more intelligent than the rest of us, have mastered problems as difficult as those that now baffle you."

—William Feather

LADIES...

"A lady is a woman who makes a man behave like a gentleman."

—Russell Lynes

"A lady is one who never shows her underwear unintentionally."

—Lillian Day

"Being powerful is like being a lady. If you have to tell people you are, you aren't."

—Margaret Thatcher

"The word LADY: Most often used to describe someone you wouldn't want to talk to for even five minutes."

—Fran Lebowitz

I wish I could drink like a lady
I can take one or two at the most
Three and I'm under the table
Four and I'm under the host

—Dorothy Parker

"A beautiful lady is an accident of nature. A beautiful old lady is a work of art."

—Louis Nizer

...AND GENTLEMEN

"A gentleman is one who never hurts anyone's feelings unintentionally."

—Oscar Wilde

"A gentleman is one who puts more into the world than he takes out."

—George Bernard Shaw

"A gentleman is simply a patient wolf."

—Lana Turner

"A gentleman with a pug nose is a contradiction in terms."

—Edgar Allan Poe

"A gentleman may love like a lunatic, but not like a beast."

—François de la Rochefoucauld

"The dog is a gentleman; I hope to go to his heaven, not man's."

—Mark Twain

"I am at heart a gentleman."

—Marlene Dietrich

HUMOR ME

"Humor is just truth, only faster!"

—Gilda Radner

"A person without a sense of humor is like a wagon without springs. It's jolted by every pebble on the road."

—Henry Ward Beecher

"Humor is just another defense against the universe."

—Mel Brooks

"The kind of humor I like is the thing that makes me laugh for five seconds and think for ten minutes."

—William Davis

"And we should consider every day lost in which we have not danced at least once. And we should call every truth false which was not accompanied by at least one laugh."

—Friedrich Nietzsche

"My way of joking is to tell the truth; it's the funniest joke in the world."

—George Bernard Shaw

"Looks fade, but humor is forever—I'll take Woody Allen over Warren Beatty any day."

—Bette Midler

"No joke is old if you haven't heard it before."

—Milton Berle

FIRST THINGS FIRST

"To know when one's self is interested, is the first condition of interesting other people."

—John Morley

ON THE SUPERNATURAL

"Belief in the supernatural reflects a failure of the imagination."

—Edward Abbey

"We can see a thousand miracles around us every day. What is more supernatural than an egg yolk turning into a chicken?"

—S. Parkes Cadman

"When people believed the earth was flat, the idea of a round world scared them silly. Then they found out how the round world works. It's the same with the world of the supernatural. Until we know how it works, we'll continue to carry around this unnecessary burden of fear."

—John Markway

"Whatever the scientists may say, if we take the supernatural out of life, we leave only the unnatural."

—Amelia E. Barr

"One often hears of a horse that shivers with terror, or of a dog that howls at something a man's eyes cannot see, and men who live primitive lives where instinct does the work of reason are fully conscious of many things that we cannot perceive at all. As life becomes more orderly, more deliberate, the supernatural world sinks farther away."

—William Butler Yeats

"Houses are not haunted. We are haunted, and regardless of the architecture with which we surround ourselves, our ghosts stay with us until we ourselves are ghosts."

—Dean Koontz

THE COWBOY'S PRAYER

"Oh Lord, I reckon I'm not much just by myself. I fail to do a lot of things I ought to do. But Lord, when trails are steep and passes high, help me to ride it straight the whole way through. And when in the falling dusk I get the final call, I do not care how many flowers they send—above all else the happiest trail would be for You to say to me, 'Let's ride, my friend.' Amen."

—Roy Rogers

I PRONOUNCE YOU GUILTY

"Guilt is the price we pay willingly for doing what we are going to do anyway."

—Isabelle Holland

"Guilt is perhaps the most painful companion of death."

—Coco Chanel

"Sin, guilt, neurosis—they are one and the same, the fruit of the tree of knowledge."

—Henry Miller

"He that is conscious of guilt cannot bear the innocence of others: So they will try to reduce all others to their own level."

—Charles James Fox

"The guilty catch themselves."

—proverb

"It is quite gratifying to feel guilty if you haven't done anything wrong: how noble! Whereas it is rather hard and certainly depressing to admit guilt and to repent."

—Hannah Arendt

"My guiding principle is this: guilt is never to be doubted."

—Franz Kafka

"Guilt is the gift that keeps on giving."

—Erma Bombeck

THE HABIT

"Habits are the nursery of errors."

—Victor Hugo

"A nail is driven out by another nail. Habit is overcome by habit."

—Desiderius Erasmus

"Habit is something you can do without thinking, which is why most of us have so many of them."

—Frank Clark

"My problem lies in reconciling my gross habits with my net income."

—Errol Flynn

Habit with him was all the test of truth;
It must be right: I've done it from my youth.

—George Crabbe

"Habits are first cobwebs, then cables."

—Spanish proverb

"It's like magic. When you live by yourself, all your annoying habits are gone!"

—Merrill Markoe

THE RAP

"I hate rap music, which to me sounds like a bunch of angry men shouting, possibly because the person who was supposed to provide them with a melody never showed up."

—Dave Barry

"Rap music...sounds like somebody feeding a rhyming dictionary to a popcorn popper."

—Tom Robbins

"I hate it when the very folks who should be listening to rap music are attacking it so hard they miss the point. The point is that children and the neighborhoods—the whole country—is drowning in violence."

—Stevie Wonder

"I often thought that if there had been a good rap group around in those days, I might have chosen a career in music instead of politics."

—Richard M. Nixon

UNCLE WALTER

"Walter Cronkite was a very sexy man. I tell you, he was the Anderson Cooper of his day. He could melt my butter each and every evening. He could toast my bread on both sides. He could float my boat, row it out to sea, and wait for it to return with the tide any day of the week. Although, I'm not quite sure what that means, I do know that Walter Cronkite was a real man."

—Margaret Schmechtman

SMART MOUTH: JAMES MADISON

"That diabolical, hell-conceived principle of persecution rages among some, and to their eternal infamy the clergy can furnish their quota of imps for such a business."

"The truth is, all men having power ought to be mistrusted."

"A government that does not trust its law-abiding citizens to keep and bear arms is itself unworthy of trust."

"A standing army is one of the greatest mischiefs that can possibly happen."

"If men were angels, no government would be necessary."

RICH MAN...

"The rich are the scum of the earth in every country."

—G. K. Chesterton

"Being rich is having money; being wealthy is having time."

—Margaret Bonnano

"If you want to know what God thinks of money, just look at the people he gave it to."

—Dorothy Parker

"In bad times, the rich usually get richer."

—Stuart Wilde

"If all the rich people in the world divided up their money among themselves, there wouldn't be enough to go around."

—Christina Stead

...POOR MAN

"Poverty is like punishment for a crime you didn't commit."

—Eli Khamarov

"Poverty is the worst form of violence."

—Mohandas K. Gandhi

"Religion is what keeps the poor man from murdering the rich."

—Napoléon Bonaparte

"Anyone who has struggled with poverty knows how extremely expensive it is to be poor."

—James Baldwin

"We have grown literally afraid to be poor. We despise anyone who elects to be poor in order to simplify and save his inner life. If he does not join the general scramble and pant with the money-making street, we deem him spiritless and lacking in ambition."

—William James

LESSON NUMBER ONE...

"The bagpipes sound exactly the same when you have finished learning as when you start."

—Thomas Beecham

QUOTES THAT KILL

"Probably the toughest time in anyone's life is when you have to murder a loved one because they're the devil."

—Emo Philips

"The fastest way to a man's heart is through his chest."

—Roseanne Barr

"Be wary of strong drink. It can make you shoot at tax collectors...and miss."

—Robert A. Heinlein

"Murder is not the crime of criminals, but that of law-abiding citizens."

—Emmanuel Teney

"Murder is commoner among cooks than among members of any other profession."

—W. H. Auden

"The very emphasis of the commandment 'Thou shalt not kill' makes it certain that we are descended from an endlessly long chain of generations of murderers, whose love of murder was in their blood as it is perhaps also in ours."

—Sigmund Freud

"Murder is always a mistake. One should never do anything that one cannot talk about after dinner."

—Oscar Wilde

GENIUS!

"Genius is only childhood recovered at will, childhood now gifted to express itself with the faculties of manhood and with the analytic mind that allows him to give order to the heap of unwittingly hoarded material."

—Charles Baudelaire

CHAPTER 5

ON FAITH

"Even the upper end of the river believes in the ocean."

—William Stafford

ON THE ROAD

"Like all great travelers I have seen more than I remember and remember more than I have seen."

—Benjamin Disraeli

"There are no foreign lands. It is the traveler only who is foreign."

—Robert Louis Stevenson

"Tourism is the vital function of the idle."

—Sergei Dovlatov

"The whole object of travel is not to set foot on foreign land; it is at last to set foot on one's own country as a foreign land."

—G. K. Chesterton

"The worst thing about being a tourist is having other tourists recognize you as a tourist."

—Russell Bake

"If you look like your passport picture, you're too ill to travel."

—Will Kommen

"I would like to spend my whole life traveling, if I could borrow another life to spend at home."

—William Hazlitt

COW NOW

"Cows are amongst the gentlest of breathing creatures; none show more passionate tenderness to their young when deprived of them; and, in short, I am not ashamed to profess a deep love for these quiet creatures."

—Thomas de Quincey

TWO FOR TODAY

"I think it truth that a life uncommanded now is uncommanded; a life unenjoyed now is unenjoyed; a life not lived wisely now is not lived wisely; for the past is gone and no one knows the future."

—David Grayson

"Let us rise up and be thankful, for if we didn't learn a lot today, at least we learned a little, and if we didn't learn a little, at least we didn't get sick, and if we got sick, at least we didn't die; so, let us all be thankful."

—Buddha

GROWING PAINS

"Middle age is when you're sitting at home on a Saturday night and the telephone rings and you hope it isn't for you."

—Ogden Nash

"Middle age is when anything new in the way you feel is most likely a symptom."

—Laurence J. Peter

"The really frightening thing about middle age is the knowledge you'll grow out of it."

—Doris Day

"Middle age is the time when a man is always thinking in a week or two he will feel as good as ever."

—Don Marquis

"I wouldn't mind being called middle-aged if only I knew a few more hundred-year-old people."

—Dean Martin

"The clothes of your life start to fit in middle age."

—Sean Penn

"Childhood is the time of life when you make faces in a mirror. Middle age is when the mirror gets even."

—Mickey Mansfield

"One of the many things nobody ever tells you about middle age is that it's such a nice change from being young."

—William Feather

HMMM...

"When I buy cookies I eat just four and throw the rest away. But first I spray them with Raid so I won't dig them out of the garbage later. Be careful, though, because Raid really doesn't taste that bad."

—Janette Barber

SMART MOUTH: MORRISSEY

"Bob Geldof is a nauseating character. Band Aid was the most self-righteous platform ever in the history of popular music."

"I think I must be, absolutely, a total sex object. In every sense of the word."

"I can get incredibly erotic about blotting paper."

"Yes, I have had a tan, actually. I went to Los Angeles and got one there, but it didn't make it back to Britain. You're not allowed to come through customs with a tan."

"I was never young. This idea of fun: cars, girls, Saturday night, bottle of wine...to me, these things are morbid. I was always attracted to people with the same problems as me. It doesn't help when most of them are dead."

"I do maintain that if your hair is wrong, your entire life is wrong."

"Nothing is important, so people, realizing that, should get on with their lives, go mad, take their clothes off, jump in the canal, jump into one of those supermarket trolleys, race around the supermarket, and steal Mars bars and kiss kittens."

YOU'VE GOT A FRIEND

"She is a friend of mind. She gather me, man. The pieces I am, she gather them and give them back to me in all the right order. It's good, you know, when you got a woman who is a friend of your mind."

—Toni Morrison

"I am thankful for the mess to clean after a party because it means I have been surrounded by friends."

—Nancie J. Carmody

"Never refuse any advance of friendship, for if nine out of ten bring you nothing, one alone may repay you."

—Madame de Tencin

"The bird a nest, the spider a web, man friendship."

—William Blake

"Without friends no one would choose to live, though he had all other goods."

—Aristotle

"A friend will help you move. A best friend will help you move...a body."

—Dave Attell

"The friend who can be silent with us in a moment of despair or confusion, who can stay with us in an hour of grief and bereavement, who can tolerate not knowing, not curing, not healing, and face with us the reality of our powerlessness, that is a friend who cares."

—Henri Nouwen

CHEERS?

"Everyone who drinks is not a poet. Some of us drink because we're not poets."

—Arthur (Dudley Moore), *Arthur* (1981)

OH VERY YOUNG...

"We could never have loved the earth so well if we had had no childhood in it."

—George Eliot

"The real menace in dealing with a five-year-old is that in no time at all you begin to sound like a five-year-old."

—Jean Kerr

"When you finally go back to your old hometown, you find it wasn't the old home you missed but your childhood."

—Sam Ewing

"I love children, especially when they cry, for then someone takes them away."

—Nancy Mitford

"Childhood is that wonderful time of life when all you need to do to lose weight is take a bath."

—Anonymous

"It is never too late to have a happy childhood."

—Tom Robbins

THREE FUNNELS

"Instead of looking at life as a narrowing funnel, we can see it ever widening to choose the things we want to do, to take the wisdom we've learned and create something."

—Liz Carpenter

"Documentary films are created in an inverted funnel of declining possibility."

—Alain Vais

"Let your head be more than a funnel to your stomach."

—German proverb

SMART MOUTH: RITA RUDNER

"I admire the pope. I have a lot of respect for anyone who can tour without an album."

"They usually have two tellers in my local bank, except when it's very busy, when they have one."

"I wonder if other dogs think poodles are members of a weird religious cult."

"I love being married. It's so great to find that one special person you want to annoy for the rest of your life."

"Neurotics build castles in the air, psychotics live in them. My mother cleans them."

"The word 'aerobics' came about when the gym instructors got together and said: If we're going to charge $10 an hour, we can't call it 'Jumping up and down.'"

"These big birthday parties my friends make for their kids: One of my friends had a surprise birthday party for her child. He was one year old. We all snuck around the crib, jumped up, and yelled, 'Surprise!' He's in therapy now."

"I got kicked out of ballet class because I pulled a groin muscle. It wasn't mine."

A DEEP THOUGHT

"Illusions commend themselves to us because they save us pain and allow us to enjoy pleasure instead. We must therefore accept it without complaint when they sometimes collide with a bit of reality against which they are dashed to pieces."

—**Sigmund Freud**

A DEEPER THOUGHT

"There are men who can think no deeper than a fact."

—**Voltaire**

A CREEP THOUGHT

"What if a demon were to creep after you one night, in your lone-liest loneliness, and say, 'This life which you live must be lived by you once again and innumerable times more; and every pain and joy and thought and sigh must come again to you, all in the same sequence. The eternal hourglass will again and again be turned and you with it, dust of the dust!' Would you throw your-self down and gnash your teeth and curse that demon? Or would you answer, 'Never have I heard anything more divine'?"

—Friedrich Nietzsche

ON WRITING

"Writing has laws of perspective, of light and shade, just as painting does, or music. If you are born knowing them, fine. If not, learn them. Then rearrange the rules to suit yourself."

—Truman Capote

"A writer is somebody for whom writing is more difficult than it is for other people."

—Thomas Mann

"The difference between the right and the nearly right word is the same as that between lightning and the lightning bug."

—Mark Twain

"One ought only to write when one leaves a piece of one's own flesh in the inkpot, each time one dips one's pen."

—Leo Tolstoy

"No passion in the world is equal to the passion to alter someone else's draft."

—H. G. Wells

"It's not plagiarism—I'm recycling words, as any good environmentally conscious writer would do."

—Uniek Swain

"The writer must believe that what he is doing is the most important thing in the world. And he must hold to this illusion even when he knows it is not true."

—John Steinbeck

FAME, FAME, FAME, FAME...

"A celebrity is one who works hard all his life to become well-known and then goes through streets wearing dark glasses so no one recognizes him."

—Fred Allen

"What is fame? The advantage of being known by people of whom you yourself know nothing, and for whom you care as little."

—Lord Byron

"Looking at the proliferation of personal web pages on the net, it looks like very soon everyone on earth will have fifteen megabytes of fame."

—M. G. Siriam

"I may be a living legend, but that sure don't help when I've got to change a tire."

—Roy Orbison

"Talent is God-given. Be humble. Fame is man-given. Be grateful. Conceit is self-given. Be careful."

—John Wooden

WINNERS' CIRCLE

"Victory goes to the player who makes the next-to-last mistake."

—Savielly Grigorievitch Tartakower

"In real life, of course, it is the hare who wins. Every time. Look around you. And in any case it is my contention that Aesop was writing for the tortoise market…Hares have no time to read. They are too busy winning the game."

—Anita Brookner

"Chemistry is B.S. I'll tell you what gives you good chemistry: winning. Losing gives you bad chemistry."

—Mike Piazza

ONE FOR WONDER

"Wonder, connected with a principle of rational curiosity, is the source of all knowledge and discovery, and it is a principle even of piety; but wonder which ends in wonder, and is satisfied with wonder, is the quality of an idiot."

—Samuel Horsley

DON'T!

"Don't tell your friends about your indigestion. 'How are you' is a greeting, not a question."

—Arthur Guiterman

"Don't worry about the world coming to an end today. It's already tomorrow in Australia."

—Charles Schulz

"Don't go to sleep. So many people die there."

—Mark Twain

"Don't discuss yourself, for you are bound to lose: if you belittle yourself, you are believed; if you praise yourself, you are disbelieved."

—Michel de Montaigne

"Don't try to perform beyond your abilities—but never perform below them."

—Frank Robinson

"Don't dig for water under the outhouse."

—Cowboy proverb

"Don't knock the weather; nine-tenths of the people couldn't start a conversation if it didn't change once in a while."

—Kin Hubbard

HE SAID, SHE SAID

"I don't like to cook. I think it's a woman's place to do the cooking. I'll go this far: I'll light the barbecue for my wife if she wants to fix steaks. When it gets right down to it, I can probably fix them better than she does, but I'd rather have her do it."

—Glen Campbell

"God made man and then said, 'I can do better than that,' and made woman."

—Adela Rogers St. Johns

"Women are like elephants to me: nice to look at, but I wouldn't want to own one."

—W. C. Fields

"Whatever women must do they must do twice as well as men to be thought half as good. Luckily, this is not too difficult."

—Charlotte Whitton

"I always get along fine with my women, as soon as they recognize that I am God."

—John Derek

"If they can put one man on the moon, why can't they put them all there?"

—Chocolate Waters

"Women's intuition is the result of millions of years of not thinking."

—Rupert Hughes

"Men are like a fine wine. They all start out like grapes, and it's our job to stomp on them and keep them in the dark until they mature into something you'd like to have dinner with."

—Kathleen Mifs

THE PARENT TRAP

"My mom always said, 'Keep your chin up.' That's how I ran into the door."

—**Daryl Hogue**

"My mom used to say it doesn't matter how many kids you have…because one kid'll take up a hundred percent of your time, so more kids can't possibly take up more than a hundred percent of your time."

—**Karen Brown**

"Whenever anything went wrong in my life, my mother would say, 'All things happen for the best.' And I'd ask, 'Whose best?' And she'd say, 'Gotta go.'"

—**Rita Rudner**

"My father used to play with my brother and me in the yard. Mother would come out and say, 'You're tearing up the grass.' 'We're not raising grass,' Dad would reply. 'We're raising boys.'"

—**Harmon Killebrew**

"My father told me all about the birds and the bees, the liar—I went steady with a woodpecker till I was twenty-one."

—**Bob Hope**

MMM...

"Life expectancy would grow by leaps and bounds if green vegetables smelled as good as bacon."

—**Doug Larson**

THE END, PART ONE

"The trouble with quotes about death is that 99.99 percent of them are made by people who are still alive."

—Joshua Bruns

"No matter how big you get, the size of your funeral depends on the weather."

—Roger Miller

Death is a Dialogue between
The Spirit and the Dust.
'Dissolve' says Death—The Spirit 'Sir
I have another Trust'—

Death doubts it—Argues from the Ground—
The Spirit turns away
Just laying off for evidence
An Overcoat of Clay.

—Emily Dickinson

"Many an ancient lord's last words have been, 'You can't kill me because I've got magic *aaargh*.'"

—Terry Pratchett

"Dying is the most embarrassing thing that can ever happen to you, because someone else has got to take care of all your details."

—Andy Warhol

"Death will be a great relief. No more interviews."

—Katharine Hepburn

FISH STORIES

"People who fish for food, and sport be damned, are called pot-fishermen. The more expert ones are called crack pot-fishermen. All other fishermen are called crackpot fishermen. This is confusing."

—Ed Zern

"My biggest worry is that when I'm dead and gone, my wife will sell my fishing gear for what I said I paid for it."

—Koos Brandt

"Lots of people committed crimes during the year who would not have done so if they'd been fishing. The increase of crime is among those deprived of the regenerations that impregnate the mind and character of the fisherman."

—Herbert Hoover

"Calling fishing a hobby is like calling brain surgery a job."

—Paul Schullery

"I fish, therefore I lie."

—Tom Clark

"There is no greater fan of fly fishing than the worm."

—Patrick McManus

"Last year I went fishing with Salvador Dali. He was using a dotted line. He caught every other fish."

—Steven Wright

"Give a man a fish and you feed him for a day. Teach a man to fish and you get rid of him on weekends."

—Nancy Gray

> Enjoy thy stream, O harmless fish;
> And when an angler for his dish,
> Through gluttony's vile sin,
> Attempts, the wretch, to pull thee out,
> God give thee strength, O gentle trout,
> To pull the rascal in!

—John Wolcot

"If people concentrated on the really important things in life, there'd be a shortage of fishing poles."

—Doug Larson

"The best way to a fisherman's heart is through his fly."

—Anonymous

CHAPTER 6

HOW TO EAT A BAGEL

"The bagel is a lonely roll to eat all by yourself because in order for the true taste to come out you need your family. One to cut the bagels, one to toast them, one to put on the cream cheese and the lox, one to put them on the table, and one to supervise."

—Gertrude Berg

EVERYONE'S A CRITIC

"Any fool can criticize, and many of them do."

—Cyril Garbett

"Asking a working writer what he thinks about critics is like asking a lamppost what it feels about dogs."

—John Osborne

"Don't pay any attention to the critics—don't even ignore them."

—Samuel Goldwyn

"Unless the bastards have the courage to give you unqualified praise, I say ignore them."

—John Steinbeck

"Criticism is often not a science; it is a craft, requiring more good health than wit, more hard work than talent, more habit than native genius. In the hands of a man who has read widely but lacks judgment, applied to certain subjects it can corrupt both its readers and the writer himself."

—Jean de la Bruyère

"Critics are like eunuchs in a harem: they know how it's done, they've seen it done every day, but they're unable to do it themselves."

—Brendan Behan

SMART MOUTH: ABIGAIL ADAMS

"Do not put such unlimited power into the hands of the husbands. Remember all men would be tyrants if they could."

"If particular care and attention is not paid to the ladies, we are determined to foment a rebellion, and will not hold ourselves bound by any laws in which we have no voice or representation."

"I've always felt that a person's intelligence is directly reflected by the number of conflicting points of view he can entertain simultaneously on the same topic."

"These are times in which a genius would wish to live. It is not in the still calm of life, or the repose of a pacific station, that great characters are formed."

"A little of what you call frippery is very necessary towards looking like the rest of the world."

HE'S NOT THERE

As I was going up the stair
I saw a man who wasn't there
He wasn't there again today
Oh, how I wish he'd go away

When I came home last night at three
The man was waiting there for me
But when I looked around the hall
I couldn't see him there at all!
Go away, go away, don't you come back any more!
Go away, go away, and please don't slam the door

Last night I saw upon the stair
A little man who wasn't there
He wasn't there again today
Oh, how I wish he'd go away

—Hugh Mearns, "Antigonish,"
from his 1899 play *Psycho-ed*

UNCLE ALBERT

"Constant kindness can accomplish much. As the sun makes ice melt, kindness causes misunderstanding, mistrust, and hostility to evaporate."

—Albert Schweitzer

TWO FOR TOOTLE

"But Noodynaady's actual ingrate tootle is of come into the garner mauve and thy nice are stores of morning and buy me a bunch of iodines."

—James Joyce, *Finnegans Wake*

"Bang-whang-whang goes the drum, tootle-tetootle the fife; No keeping one's haunches still: it's the greatest pleasure in life."

—Robert Browning

LEFT, RIGHT, LEFT, RIGHT...

"A liberal is a man who leaves the room when the fight begins."

—Heywood Hale Broun

"Conservatives are not necessarily stupid, but most stupid people are conservative."

—John Stuart Mill

"If God had been a liberal, we wouldn't have had the Ten Commandments—we'd have the Ten Suggestions."

—Malcolm Bradbury

"If the Republicans will stop telling lies about us, we will stop telling the truth about them."

—Adlai Stevenson

"A liberal is a man too broad-minded to take his own side in a quarrel."

—Robert Frost

"A conservative is one who admires radicals centuries after they're dead."

—Leo Rosten

"A liberal is a person whose interests aren't at stake at the moment."

—Willis Player

"A conservative is a man who just sits and thinks, mostly sits."

—Woodrow Wilson

IT ALL ADDS UP

"The cowboys have a way of trussing up a steer or a pugnacious bronco which fixes the brute so that it can neither move nor think. This is the hog-tie, and it is what Euclid did to geometry."

—Eric T. Bell

"317 is a prime, not because we think so, or because our minds are shaped in one way rather than another, but because it is so. Mathematical reality is built that way."

—Godfrey Hardy

"I know that two and two make four—and should be glad to prove it, too, if I could—though I must say if by any sort of process I could convert two and two into five, it would give me much greater pleasure."

—Lord Byron

There was a young man from Trinity,
Who solved the square root of infinity.
While counting the digits,
He was seized by the fidgets,
Dropped science, and took up divinity.

—Anonymous

Professor: "If I gave you a dollar and your father gave you a dollar, how much would you have?"
Larry: "One dollar."
Professor: "You don't know your arithmetic."
Larry: "You don't know my father.

—The Three Stooges, *The Half-Wits Holiday* (1947)

"Can you do Division? Divide a loaf by a knife—what's the answer to that?"

—Lewis Carroll, *Through the Looking-Glass*

"As long as there is algebra, there will be prayer in school."

—Larry Miller

NEVER...

"Never trouble another for what you can do for yourself."

—Thomas Jefferson

"Never trust a man with short legs. Brains too near their bottoms."

—Noël Coward

"Never attribute to malice what can adequately be explained by stupidity."

—Nick Diamos

"Never have a friend that's poorer than yourself."

—Douglas Jerrold

"Never cut what you can untie."

—Joseph Joubert

"Never trust the teller. Trust the tale."

—D. H. Lawrence

"Never go to bed mad. Stay up and fight."

—Phyllis Diller

THE DARWIN LORDS?

"Upon seeing the marsupials in Australia for the first time and comparing them to placental mammals: An unbeliever...might exclaim, 'Surely two distinct Creators must have been at work.'"

—Charles Darwin

THE PHILOSOPHER'S TONE

"To teach how to live without certainty and yet without being paralyzed by hesitation is perhaps the chief thing that philosophy, in our age, can do for those who study it."

—Bertrand Russell

"It was previously a question of finding out whether or not life had to have a meaning to be lived. It now becomes clear, on the contrary, that it will be lived all the better if it has no meaning."

—Albert Camus

"It is the path of least resistance that makes rivers and men crooked."

—B. J. Palmer

"Never let your sense of morals keep you from doing what is right."

—Isaac Asimov

"Among the facts of the universe to be accounted for, it may be said, is Mind; and it is self-evident that nothing can have produced Mind but Mind."

—John Stuart Mill

"All are lunatics, but he who can analyze his delusion is called a philosopher."

—Ambrose Bierce

HAVE ANOTHER BEER QUOTE

"The mouth of a perfectly happy man is filled with beer."

—Egyptian proverb

"God has a brown voice, as soft and full as beer."

—Anne Sexton

"I am a firm believer in the people. If given the truth, they can be depended upon to meet any national crisis. The great point is to bring them the real facts, and beer."

—Abraham Lincoln

"Here's to a long life and a merry one; a quick death and an easy one; a pretty girl and a true one; a cold beer, and another one."

—Lewis Henry

"I was at a bar nursing a beer. My nipple was getting quite soggy."

—Emo Philips

"Life, alas, is very drear. Up with the glass! Down with the beer!"

—Louis Untermeyer

SMART MOUTH: ANAÏS NIN

"I know why families were created, with all their imperfections. They humanize you. They are made to make you forget yourself occasionally, so that the beautiful balance of life is not destroyed."

"Each contact with a human being is so rare, so precious, one should preserve it."

"There is not one big cosmic meaning for all; there is only the meaning we each give to our life, an individual meaning, an individual plot, like an individual novel, a book for each person."

"The possession of knowledge does not kill the sense of wonder and mystery. There is always more mystery."

"When you make a world tolerable for yourself, you make a world tolerable for others."

"I, with a deeper instinct, choose a man who compels my strength, who makes enormous demands on me, who does not doubt my courage or my toughness, who does not believe me naive or innocent, who has the courage to treat me like a woman."

"We don't see things as they are, we see them as we are."

"And the day came when the risk to remain tight in a bud was more painful than the risk it took to blossom."

HMMM...

"I told people I was a drummer before I even had a set. I was a mental drummer."

—**Keith Moon**

LES MISÉRABLES

"Misery is almost always the result of thinking."

—**Joseph Joubert**

"Friends love misery, in fact. Sometimes, especially if we are too lucky or too successful or too pretty, our misery is the only thing that endears us to our friends."

—**Erica Jong**

"It is by attempting to reach the top in a single leap that so much misery is caused in the world."

—**William Cobbett**

"It's been a misery for me, living with Christine Keeler."

—**Christine Keeler**

"Money can't buy you happiness, but it does bring you a more pleasant form of misery."

—**Spike Milligan**

"Don Juan assured me that in order to accomplish the feat of making myself miserable I had to work in a most intense fashion, and that it was absurd…'The trick is in what one emphasizes,' he said. We either make ourselves miserable, or we make ourselves strong. The amount of work is the same."

—**Carlos Castaneda**

"As our life is very short, so it is very miserable, and therefore it is well it is short."

—**Bishop Jeremy Taylor**

EGGZACTLY

"Thy head is as full of quarrels as an egg is full of meat, and yet thy head hath been beaten as addle as an egg for quarreling."

—**William Shakespeare**, *Romeo and Juliet*

"I've met a lot of hard-boiled eggs in my time, but you're twenty minutes."

—**Billy Wilder**

"When arguing with a stone, an egg is always wrong."

—**African proverb**

COMPUTATIONS

"The computing field is always in need of new clichés."

—Alan Perlis

"Why is it drug addicts and computer aficionados are both called users?"

—Clifford Stoll

"You can't fail to get along with a computer; it will never turn upon you, it will never insist on talking about what it wants to or doing what it wants to. It will never find you boring, never forget to call, never ask for a favor."

—Greg Easterbrook

"Part of the inhumanity of the computer is that, once it is competently programmed and working smoothly, it is completely honest."

—Isaac Asimov

"Computers are like Old Testament gods; lots of rules and no mercy."

—Joseph Campbell

"Imagine if every Thursday your shoes exploded if you tied them the usual way. This happens to us all the time with computers, and nobody thinks of complaining."

—Jef Raskin

"Computers are useless. They only give you answers."

—Pablo Picasso

PUNCH AND JUDY

"Shoplifting is a victimless crime. Like punching someone in the dark."

—Nelson Muntz, *The Simpsons*

"Behind every cloud is another cloud."

—Judy Garland

"An attempt at visualizing the Fourth Dimension: Take a point, stretch it into a line, curl it into a circle, twist it into a sphere, and punch through the sphere."

—Albert Einstein

"Most artwork comes out of someplace you can just tap into, and make that so obvious. And then other people can look at it and say, 'I know that place too, that craving.'"

—Judy Pfaff

"At least the Pilgrim Fathers used to shoot Indians: the Pilgrim Children merely punch time clocks."

—E. E. Cummings

"Don't spit on my cupcake and tell me it's frosting."

—Judge Judy

"That the way to do it!"

—Punch, *Punch and Judy*

SPIDER/MAN

"The means to gain happiness is to throw out from oneself like a spider in all directions an adhesive web of love, and to catch in it all that comes."

—Leo Tolstoy

SMART MOUTH: JON STEWART

"You have to remember one thing about the will of the people: it wasn't that long ago that we were swept away by the Macarena."

"The nation of Dubai banned the movie *Charlie's Angels* because it's 'offensive to the religion of Islam.' Apparently, the religion of Islam is offended by anything without a plot."

"Alright guys, I want you to get out there and vote tomorrow. And not because it's cool, because it's not. You know what is cool? Smoking. Smoke while you vote."

"Thou shall not kill. Thou shall not commit adultery. Don't eat pork. I'm sorry, what was that last one? Don't eat pork. God has spoken. Is that the word of God or is that pigs trying to outsmart everybody?"

"News used to hold itself to a higher plane and slowly it has dissolved into, well, me."

"In 1981 I lost my virginity, only to gain it back again on appeal in 1983."

"I heard Dennis Kucinich say in a debate, 'When I'm president...' and I just wanted to stop him and say, 'Dude.'"

QUOTATIONS COURAGEOUS

"Courage is the ladder on which all the other virtues mount."

—Claire Booth Luce

"Courageousness is a way of death, not life."

—Gabriel Laub

"The test of courage comes when we are in the minority. The test of tolerance comes when we are in the majority."

—Ralph W. Sockman

"Be sure to put your feet in the right place. Then stand firm."

—Abraham Lincoln

"Courage without conscience is a wild beast."

—Robert G. Ingersoll

"Life is mainly froth and bubble / Two things stand like stone— Kindness in another's trouble. / Courage in your own."

—Adam Lindsay Gordon

I'D RATHER...

"I'd rather have ten snakes in the house than one fly."

—Mark Twain

"WOOF!"

"Dogs have more love than integrity. They've been true to us, yes, but they haven't been true to themselves."

—Clarence Day

"A dog's best friend is his illiteracy."

—Ogden Nash

"To his dog, every man is Napoléon; hence the constant popularity of dogs."

—Aldous Huxley

"There is no psychiatrist in the world like a puppy licking your face."

—Ben Williams

"Even a little dog can piss on a big building."

—Jim Hightower

"I loathe people who keep dogs. They are cowards who haven't got the guts to bite people themselves."

—August Strindberg

"A dog teaches a boy fidelity, perseverance, and to turn around three times before lying down."

—Robert Benchley

"If a dog will not come to you after having looked you in the face, you should go home and examine your conscience."

—Woodrow Wilson

"If you're a dog and your owner suggests that you wear a sweater, suggest that he wear a tail."

—Fran Lebowitz

CHAPTER 7

NAKED LUNCH

"Las Vegas is Everyman's cut-rate Babylon. Not far away there is, or was, a roadside lunch counter and over it a sign proclaiming in three words that a Roman emperor's orgy is now a democratic institution: 'Topless Pizza Lunch.'"

—Alistair Cooke

SMART MOUTH:
HUNTER S. THOMPSON

"The music business is a cruel and shallow money trench, a long plastic hallway where thieves and pimps run free, and good men die like dogs. There's also a negative side."

"I feel the same way about disco as I do about herpes."

"If I'd written all the truth I knew for the past ten years, about 600 people—including me—would be rotting in prison cells from Rio to Seattle today. Absolute truth is a very rare and dangerous commodity in the context of professional journalism."

"Call on God, but row away from the rocks."

"That was always the difference between Muhammad Ali and the rest of us. He came, he saw, and if he didn't entirely conquer—he came as close as anybody we are likely to see in the lifetime of this doomed generation."

"Weird heroes and mould-breaking champions exist as living proof to those who need it that the tyranny of 'the rat race' is not yet final."

"I hate to advocate drugs, alcohol, violence, or insanity to anyone, but they've always worked for me."

AFTERTHOUGHT

"We exaggerate misfortune and happiness alike. We are never as bad off or as happy as we say we are."
—Honoré de Balzac

FYVE QWOTES

"'Correct' spelling, indeed, is one of the arts that are far more esteemed by schoolma'ams than by practical men, neck-deep in the heat and agony of the world."
—H. L. Mencken

"My spelling is Wobbly. It's good spelling but it Wobbles, and the letters get in the wrong places."
—A. A. Milne

"Take care that you never spell a word wrong. Always before you write a word, consider how it is spelled, and, if you do not remember, turn to a dictionary. It produces great praise to a lady to spell well."

—Thomas Jefferson, to his daughter

"A man must be a great fool who can't spell a word more than one way."

—Marshall Brown

"I have a correspondent whose letters are always a refreshment to me, there is such a breezy unfettered originality about his orthography. He always spells Kow with a large K. Now that is just as good as to spell it with a small one. It is better. It gives the imagination a broader field, a wider scope. It suggests to the mind a grand, vague, impressive new kind of a cow."

—Mark Twain

ON EDUCATION

"What does education often do? It makes a straight-cut ditch out of a free, meandering brook."

—Henry David Thoreau

"Good teaching is one-quarter preparation and three-quarters theater."

—Gail Godwin

"Men are born ignorant, not stupid; they are made stupid by education."

—Bertrand Russell

"Education is a state-controlled manufactory of echoes."

—Norman Douglas

"Education is what survives when what has been learned has been forgotten."

—B. F. Skinner

"To teach is to learn twice."

—Joseph Joubert

"The highest result of education is tolerance."

—Helen Keller

FOUR

"If you're respectful by habit, constantly honoring the worthy, four things increase: long life, beauty, happiness, strength."

—Buddha

"There are four ways, and only four ways, in which we have contact with the world. We are evaluated and classified by these four contacts: what we do, how we look, what we say, and how we say it."

—Dale Carnegie

"When angry, count to four. When very angry, swear."

—Mark Twain

"A man loses his sense of direction after four drinks; a woman loses hers after four kisses."

—H. L. Mencken

FORE!

"I'm into golf now. I'm getting pretty good. I can almost hit the ball as far as I can throw the clubs."

—Bob Ettinger

"I love wearing the clothes. The golf course is the only place I can go dressed like a pimp and fit in perfectly. Anywhere else, lime-green pants and alligator shoes, and I got a cop on my ass."

—Samuel L. Jackson

"It's easy to see golf not as a game at all but as some whey-faced, nineteenth-century Presbyterian minister's fever dream of exorcism achieved through ritual and self-mortification."

—Bruce McCall

"Golf and sex are the only things you can enjoy without being good at it."

—Jimmy Demaret

"Golf appeals to the idiot in us and the child. Just how childlike golf players become is proven by their frequent inability to count past five."

—John Updike

"The number of shots taken by an opponent who is out of sight is equal to the square root of the sum of the number of curses heard plus the number of swishes."

—Michael Green

"I played golf. I didn't get a hole in one, but I did hit a guy. That's way more satisfying."

—Mitch Hedberg

A THING AS LOVELY

"The scarlet of the maples can shake me like a cry,
Of bugles going by."

—William Bliss Carman

OH, CANADA

"Canadians are the people who learned to live without the bold accents of the natural ego-trippers of other lands."

—Marshall McLuhan

"Canadians have been so busy explaining to the Americans that we aren't British, and to the British that we aren't Americans, that we haven't had time to become Canadians."

—Helen Gordon McPherson

Canada could have enjoyed:
English government,
French culture,
And American know-how.
Instead it ended up with:
English know-how,
French government,
And American culture.

—John Robert Colombo

"Canadians are generally indistinguishable from Americans and the surest way to tell the two apart is to make this observation to a Canadian."

—Richard Starnes

"There are few, if any, Canadian men that have never spelled their name in a snow bank."

—Douglas Coupland

"Canada is a country so square that even the female impersonators are women."

—Richard Brenner

ON TELEVISION

"Television is a medium of entertainment which permits millions of people to listen to the same joke at the same time, and yet remain lonesome."

—T. S. Eliot

"Television has proved that people will look at anything rather than each other."

—Ann Landers

"It's a strange thing, this television. God didn't design anyone to be recognized by two billion people."

—Peter Falk

"The only way to get any feeling from a television set is to touch it when you're wet."

—Larry Gelbart

"Television: chewing gum for the eyes."

—Frank Lloyd Wright

"How can you put on a meaningful drama when, every fifteen minutes, proceedings are interrupted by twelve dancing rabbits with toilet paper?"

—Rod Serling

THE TRUTH

"And if all others accepted the lie which the Party imposed—if all records told the same tale—then the lie passed into history and became truth. 'Who controls the past' ran the Party slogan, 'controls the future: who controls the present controls the past.'"

—George Orwell, 1984

∃ƆИA⅃UᙠMA

"I was in front of an ambulance the other day, and I noticed that the word 'ambulance' was spelled in reverse print on the hood of the ambulance. And I thought, 'Well, isn't that clever.' I look in the rear-view mirror, I can read the word 'ambulance' behind me. Of course while you're reading, you don't see where you're going, you crash, you need an ambulance. I think they're trying to drum up some business on the way back from lunch."

—Jerry Seinfeld

RANDOM BITS OF WISDOM

"Remember there's a big difference between kneeling down and bending over."

—Frank Zappa

"Always tell the truth —it's the easiest thing to remember."

—David Mamet

"Learn all the rules, every one of them, so that you will know how to break them."

—Irvin S. Cobb

"Beginnings are usually scary and endings are usually sad, but it's the middle that counts. You have to remember this when you find yourself at the beginning."

—Sandra Bullock

"Be careful to choose your enemies well. Friends don't much matter. But the choice of enemies is very important."

—Oscar Wilde

"If opportunity doesn't knock, build a door."

—Milton Berle

YOU ARE FAMILY, PART TWO

"The family is one of nature's masterpieces."

—George Santayana

"Happy families are all alike; every unhappy family is unhappy in its own way."

—Leo Tolstoy

"Family quarrels are bitter things. They don't go by any rules. They're not like aches or wounds; they're more like splits in the skin that won't heal because there's not enough material."

—F. Scott Fitzgerald

"Important families are like potatoes. The best parts are underground."

—Francis Bacon

LIFE, THE UNIVERSE, AND A THEORY

"There is a theory that if ever anybody discovers exactly what the universe is for and why it is here, it will instantly disappear and be replaced by something even more bizarre and inexplicable. There is another theory which states that this has already happened."

—Douglas Adams

HEY, BULLDOG

Bulldogs Are Adorable
With Faces Like Toads
That Have Been Sat On

—Anonymous

SMART MOUTH: WINSTON CHURCHILL

"Man will occasionally stumble over the truth, but usually manages to pick himself up, walk over or around it, and carry on."

"Never hold discussions with the monkey when the organ grinder is in the room."

"Those who can win a war well can rarely make a good peace, and those who could make a good peace would never have won the war."

"However beautiful the strategy, you should occasionally look at the results."

"I cannot pretend to feel impartial about colors. I rejoice with the brilliant ones and am genuinely sorry for the poor browns."

"When I look back on all these worries I remember the story of the old man who said on his deathbed that he had a lot of trouble in his life, most of which had never happened."

"I am prepared to meet my Maker. Whether my Maker is prepared for the ordeal is another matter."

"By swallowing evil words unsaid, no one has ever harmed his stomach."

THE DIRECTOR'S CHAIR

"I have ten commandments. The first nine are, 'Thou shalt not bore.' The tenth is, 'Thou shalt have right of final cut.'"

—Billy Wilder

"I write scripts to serve as skeletons awaiting the flesh and sinew of images."

—Ingmar Bergman

"I think all directors should at least take acting classes and see what an actor goes through. And I think all actors should try to direct and see what a director has to go through—like we don't do it on purpose to take three hours to light the scene. I'm not thrilled with it either, but that's what it takes."

—Penny Marshall

"I made some mistakes in drama. I thought drama was when the actor cried. But drama is when the audience cries."

—Frank Capra

"Anybody can direct a picture once they know the fundamentals. Directing is not a mystery, it's not an art. The main thing about directing is: photograph the people's eyes."

—John Ford

"Choosing a cast is one of the most difficult jobs as a director. And it is also the most interesting because the decisions have to be made at a point when you know least about the movie. During the work with the cast, which I take very seriously, the foundation for how the film will turn out is settled. I receive help from the cast too, and I believe that all you have to do is to keep your ears and eyes open, then the right actor or actress will tell you what to do."

—Jane Campion

"In feature films the director is God; in documentary films God is the director."

—Alfred Hitchcock

"I steal from every movie ever made."

—Quentin Tarantino

"Movie directing is a perfect refuge for the mediocre."

—Orson Welles

THE DARK SIDE

"This is the very worst wickedness, that we refuse to acknowledge the passionate evil that is in us. This makes us secret and rotten."

—D. H. Lawrence

REMEMBER...

"Remember your humanity and forget the rest."

—Albert Einstein

"In the end, we will remember not the words of our enemies but the silence of our friends."

—Martin Luther King Jr.

"Remember, people will judge you by your actions, not your intentions. You may have a heart of gold—but so does a hard-boiled egg."

—Anonymous

"Hard though it may be to accept, remember that guilt is sometimes a friendly internal voice reminding you that you're messing up."

—Marge Kennedy

> Remember all those renowned generations,
> Remember all that have sunk in their blood,
> Remember all that have died on the scaffold,
> Remember all that have fled, that have stood,
> Stood, took death like a tune
> On an old tambourine.

—William Butler Yeats

"And always remember the last words of my grandfather, who said, 'A truck!'"

—Emo Philips

NAVEL THINKING

"A man should kiss his wife's navel every day."

—Nell Kimball

"Society was so much more prudish in the 1960s. In one episode of the Avengers I played a belly dancer and I had to stick a jewel in my navel because the Americans wouldn't tolerate them.

—Diana Rigg

"Japan has long had a special regard for the navel. The shape of the umbilicus of a newborn baby would be discussed at length, and if it happened to point downward, the parents would brace themselves for a weakling child who would bring them woe."

—"Japan: Navel Exercise," *Time*, February, 1959

HISTORY, AGAIN

"The past is not dead. In fact, it's not even past."

—William Faulkner

"History is more or less bunk."

—Henry Ford

"Half the things you've been taught in school are just convenient fictions. History is a puppet show for childish minds."

—John Twelve Hawks

"If you would understand anything, observe its beginning and its development."

—Aristotle

"History is the only laboratory we have in which to test the consequences of thought."

—Etienne Gilson

"Nothing has really happened until it has been recorded."

—Virginia Woolf

GENIUS!

"Firmness of purpose is one of the most necessary sinews of character, and one of the best instruments of success. Without it genius wastes its efforts in a maze of inconsistencies."

—Lord Chesterfield

UH-OH

"It's true that every time you hear a bell, an angel gets its wings. But what they don't tell you is that every time you hear a mouse trap snap, an angel gets set on fire."

—Jack Handey

SMART MOUTH: JOAN BAEZ

"I've been obsessed with stopping people from blowing each other's brains out since I was ten."

"If it's natural to kill, how come men have to go into training to learn how?"

"To sing is to love and affirm, to fly and soar, to coast into the hearts of the people who listen, to tell them that life is to live, that love is there, that nothing is a promise, but that beauty exists, and must be hunted for and found."

"Hypothetical questions get hypothetical answers."

"I have a sister who lives deep in the woods in Carmel Valley. To give a quick sketch of her, the other day she was taking her usual walk and she saw a mountain lion about 20 feet ahead of her. It turned around, looked at her and she said, 'Hello beastie.' I would like to think I'd be cool like that, but I wouldn't."

"I've never had a humble opinion. If you've got an opinion, why be humble about it?"

SOUNDS IMPOSSIBLE, BUT...

"Try to be better than yourself."

—**William Faulkner**

CHAPTER 8

HMMM...

"He who fights too long against dragons becomes a dragon himself; and if you gaze too long into the abyss, the abyss will gaze into you."

—Friedrich Nietzsche

FOUR FOR THE FUTURE

"The future is something which everyone reaches at the rate of sixty minutes an hour, whatever he does, whoever he is."

—C. S. Lewis

"Tomorrow, every fault is to be amended; but tomorrow never comes."

—Benjamin Franklin

"Tomorrow is the most important thing in life. Comes into us at midnight very clean. It's perfect when it arrives and it puts itself in our hands. It hopes we've learned something from yesterday."

—John Wayne

"The future always arrives too fast...and in the wrong order."

—Alvin Toffler

THAT'S MENTAL

"I think the big danger of madness is not madness itself, but the habit of madness. What I discovered during the time I spent in the asylum is that I could choose madness and spend my whole life without working, doing nothing, pretending to be mad. It was a very strong temptation."

—Paulo Coelho

"The statistics on sanity say that one out of every four Americans is suffering from mental illness. Think of your three best friends. If they're okay, then it's you."

—Rita Mae Brown

"Some people hear their own inner voices with great clearness. And they live by what they hear. Such people become crazy...or they become legend."

—Jim Harrison

"Insanity: a perfectly rational adjustment to the insane world."

—R. D. Laing

There is
A madman inside of you
Who is always running for office—
Why vote him in,
For he never keeps the accounts straight.
He gets all kinds of crooked deals
Happening all over town
That will just give you a big headache
And glue to your kisser
A gigantic
Confused
Frown.

—Hafiz

A LOVE SUPREME

"I met in the street a very poor young man who was in love. His hat was old, his coat worn, his cloak was out at the elbows, the water passed through his shoes—and the stars through his soul."

—Victor Hugo

SMART MOUTH: MITCH HEDBERG

"I don't have a girlfriend. But I do know a woman who'd be mad at me for saying that."

"I'm against picketing, but I don't know how to show it."

"I got my hair highlighted because I felt that some strands were more important than others."

"I have a cheese-shredder at home, which is its positive name. They don't call it by its negative name, which is sponge-ruiner."

"I got an ant farm. Them fellas didn't grow sh*t."

"I type 101 words a minute. But it's in my own language."

"One time a guy handed me a picture of himself and said, 'Here's a picture of me when I was younger.' Every picture of you is of when you were younger."

"I bought a doughnut and they gave me a receipt for the doughnut. I can't imagine a scenario that I would have to prove to some skeptical friend that I bought a doughnut. 'Don't even act like I didn't buy a doughnut. I've got the documentation right here.'"

"My sister wanted to be an actress, but she never made it. She does live in a trailer. She got halfway. She's an actress, she just never gets called to the set."

"This is what my friend said to me: he said, 'Guess what I like— mashed potatoes.' It's like, 'Dude. You gotta give me time to guess. If you're gonna quiz me, you must insert a pause in there.'"

"I like vending machines cause snacks are better when they fall. If I buy a candy bar at a store, oftentimes I will drop it…so that it achieves its maximum flavor potential."

THE GUITAR

"Among God's creatures two, the dog and the guitar, have taken all the sizes and all the shapes, in order to not be separated from the man."

—Andre Segovia

"It took me twenty years to learn I couldn't tune too well. And by that time I was too rich to care."

—Chet Atkins

"My vocation is more in composition really than anything else—
building up harmonies using the guitar, orchestrating the guitar
like an army, a guitar army."

—Jimmy Page

"I think I'm a habitual documenter. I think the chords I choose
are a document of where I'm at at any given time, that they
depict—if not the state I'm in at the time that I create it—at least
the companion for the story."

—Joni Mitchell

"I'm glad there are a lot of guitar players pursuing technique as
diligently as they possibly can, because it leaves this whole other
area open to people like me."

—Richard Thompson

"Every time you pick up your guitar to play, play as if it's the last
time."

—Eric Clapton

> They said, "You have a blue guitar,
> You do not play things as they are."
> The man replied, "Things as they are
> Are changed upon a blue guitar."
>
> **—Wallace Stevens**

"My guitar is not a thing. It is an extension of myself. It is who
I am."

—Joan Jett

CARDS ON THE TABLE

"I don't suffer fools gladly. I'm not here to make friends. I've learnt that the hard way. I used to not say things like 'I really want to hold a guitar in my video,' because I was trying to make everyone like me. But I don't give a sh*t now."

—Amy Winehouse

ON SUCCESS

"Success and failure are both difficult to endure. Along with success come drugs, divorce, fornication, bullying, travel, medication, depression, neurosis, and suicide. With failure comes failure."

—Joseph Heller

"I couldn't wait for success, so I went ahead without it."

—Jonathan Winters

"How far you go in life depends on you being tender with the young, compassionate with the aged, sympathetic with the striving, and tolerant of the weak and the strong. Because someday in life you will have been all of these."

—George Washington Carver

"Success is having to worry about every darned thing in the world except money."

—Johnny Cash

"The worst part about success is trying to find someone who is happy for you."

—Bette Midler

"It is not enough to succeed; others must fail."

—**Gore Vidal**

HMMM...

"A man must swallow a toad every morning if he wishes to be sure of finding nothing still more disgusting before the day is over."

—**Nicolas de Chamfort**

HE SAID, SHE SAID: PART TWO

"The great question that has never been answered, and which I have not yet been able to answer, despite my thirty years of research into the feminine soul, is 'What does a woman want?'"

—**Sigmund Freud**

"There's a commercial where guys sit around drinking beer, cleaning fish, wiping their noses on their sleeves, and saying, 'It doesn't get any better than this.' That's not a commercial. That's a warning."

—**Diane Jordan**

"Three things have been difficult to tame: the oceans, fools, and women. We may soon be able to tame the oceans; fools and women will take a little longer."

—**Spiro Agnew**

"Beware of the man who denounces women writers; his penis is tiny and he cannot spell."

—**Erica Jong**

"Women like silent men. They think they're listening."

—Marcel Achard

"He is every other inch a gentleman."

—Rebecca West

I SEE LONDON, I SEE...

"If you are lucky enough to have lived in Paris as a young man, then wherever you go for the rest of your life, it stays with you, for Paris is a moveable feast."

—Ernest Hemingway

"Frenchmen are like gunpowder, each by itself smutty and contemptible, but mass them together and they are terrible indeed!"

—Samuel Taylor Coleridge

"The French: Germans with good food."

—Fran Lebowitz

"How can you govern a country which produces 246 different kinds of cheese?"

—Charles de Gaulle

"The best of America drifts to Paris. The American in Paris is the best American. It is more fun for an intelligent person to live in an intelligent country. France has the only two things toward which we drift as we grow older—intelligence and good manners."

—F. Scott Fitzgerald

GOOD ADVICE

"Always give a word or a sign of salute when meeting or passing a friend, even a stranger, if in a lonely place."

—Tecumseh

YOU THINK?

"Experts in ancient Greek culture say that people back then didn't see their thoughts as belonging to them. When ancient Greeks had a thought, it occurred to them as a god or goddess giving an order. Apollo was telling them to be brave. Athena was telling them to fall in love. Now people hear a commercial for sour cream potato chips and rush out to buy, but now they call this free will. At least the ancient Greeks were being honest."

—Chuck Palahniuk

THE LAND OF THE FREE

"Is life so dear, or peace so sweet, as to be purchased at the price of chains and slavery? Forbid it, Almighty God! I know not what course others may take; but as for me, give me liberty or give me death!"

—Patrick Henry

"Liberty doesn't work as well in practice as it does in speeches."

—Will Rogers

"Liberty means responsibility; that is why most men dread it."

—George Bernard Shaw

"Disobedience is the true foundation of liberty. The obedient must be slaves."

—Henry David Thoreau

"We are so concerned to flatter the majority that we lose sight of how often it is necessary, in order to preserve freedom for the minority, to face that majority down."

—William F. Buckley Jr.

"The right to be let alone is indeed the beginning of all freedom."

—William O. Douglas

"Freedom is not an ideal, it is not even a protection, if it means nothing more than freedom to stagnate, to live without dreams, to have no greater aim than a second car and another television set."

—Adlai Stevenson

PROSIT!

"You sit back in the darkness, nursing your beer, breathing in that ineffable aroma of the old-time saloon: dark wood, spilled beer, good cigars, and ancient whiskey—the sacred incense of the drinking man."

—Bruce Aidells

"One tequila, two tequila, three tequila—floor."

—George Carlin

"I only drink to make other people seem interesting."

—George Jean Nathan

"I believe, if we take habitual drunkards as a class, their heads and their hearts will bear an advantageous comparison with those of any other class. There seems ever to have been a proneness in the brilliant and warm-blooded to fall into this vice."

—Abraham Lincoln

"Alcohol may be man's worst enemy, but the Bible says love your enemy."

—Frank Sinatra

"I try not to drink too much because when I'm drunk, I bite."

—Bette Midler

GOOD ADVICE

"The best time to plant a tree is twenty years ago. The second best time is now."

—Anonymous

SMART MOUTH: MAE WEST

"Too much of a good thing can be wonderful."

"Save a boyfriend for a rainy day—and another, in case it doesn't rain."

"I used to be Snow White…but I drifted."

"Give a man a free hand and he'll run it all over you."

"I may be good for nothing, but I'm never bad for nothing."

"Ten men at my door? I'm tired. Send one of them away."

"When choosing between two evils, I always like to try the one I've never tried before."

"If I asked for a cup of coffee, someone would search for the double meaning."

TO TODAY

"This day is too precious to be corroded by acid worries and vitriolic regrets. Keep your chin high and your thoughts sparkling, a mountain brook leaping in the spring sunshine. Seize this day. It will never come again."

—Dale Carnegie

FROM THE BIRDS

"What's better—dogs or broomsticks? I mean, will the world really ever know?"

—Larry Bird

"Few men during their lifetime come anywhere near exhausting the resources dwelling in them. There are deep wells of strength that are never used."

—Admiral Richard E. Byrd

"It's odd that you can get so anesthetized by your own pain or your own problem that you don't quite fully share the hell of someone close to you."

—Lady Bird Johnson

"I guess I'm always in search of the perfect song, which I don't feel like I've written yet, nor am I sure I ever will. You know, a song like The Beatles 'Yesterday.'"

—Sheryl Crow

"It's very difficult for me to dislike an artist. No matter what he's creating, the fact that he's experiencing the joy of creation makes me feel like we're in a brotherhood of some kind."

—Chick Corea

"My heroes are Larry Bird, Admiral Byrd, Lady Bird, Sheryl Crow, Chick Corea, the inventor of birdseed, and anyone who reads to you even if she's tired."

—Big Bird

MORE FAMOUS LAST WORDS

"What is the answer? In that case, what is the question?"

—Gertrude Stein (1946)

"God damn it, I knew it! Born in a hotel room and dying in a hotel room!"

—Eugene O'Neill (1953)

"You made one mistake. You married me."

—Brendan Behan (1964)

"Why not?"

—Timothy Leary (1996)

"Listen...I am singing a little song for. The whole world came between us."

—John Reed (1920)

FAMOUS LAST WORDS IN FILMS

"We train young men to drop fire on people. But their commanders won't allow them to write 'f**k' on their airplanes because it's obscene...the horror...the horror..."

—Walter Kurtz (Marlon Brando),
***Apocalypse Now* (1979)**

"Helllllllp!"

**—Skinnydipper Chrissie Watkins
(Susan Backlinie), *Jaws* (1975)**

"What is your major malfunction, numbnuts? Didn't mommy and daddy show you enough attention when you were a child?"

**— Gunnery Seargent Hartman
(R. Lee Ermey) *Full Metal Jacket* (1998)**

"What we've got here is a failure to communicate."

**—Luke (Paul Newman),
Cool Hand Luke (1967)**

"Ha ha ha ha ha! You whores, you scum, I piss in your faces !!!! Ha ha ha ha ha!!"

**—Tony Montana (Al Pacino),
Scarface (1983)**

"It's gonna be alright."

**—Clint Reno (Elvis Presley),
Love Me Tender (1956)**

"Mo Cuishla."

**—Maggie Fitzgerald (Hilary Swank),
Million Dollar Baby (2004)**

"Heaven, I'm in heaven…heaven…heaven…"

—James Coffey (Michael Clarke Duncan),
***The Shawshank Redemption* (1994)**

"WAAAAA-HOO!"

—Major T. J. "King" Kong (Slim Pickens),
***Dr. Strangelove* (1964)**

SMART MOUTH: GILDA RADNER

"Adopted kids are such a pain—you have to teach them how to look like you."

"I'm so full I can't hear."

"I can't understand how I got famous. It seemed like I just kept taking jobs, and it turned out that millions of people were suddenly watching me do it. The first time I ever saw the word 'famous,' it was on a menu in Detroit, where they said, 'Famous Chili.' Is that how famous I am?"

"Funny is the thin side of being fat."

"I could make a stab at 'gorgeous' as long as I had something funny to say to get me out of it."

"I guess in France, you don't order French fries. You just order fries. They'll know."

"I always wanted a happy ending. Now I've learned, the hard way, that some poems don't rhyme, and some stories don't have a clear beginning, middle, and end. Life is about not knowing, having to change, taking the moment, and making the best of it without knowing what's going to happen next. Delicious ambiguity."

FRIENDLY ADVICE

If you want enemies, excel your friends, but if you want friends, let your friends excel you."

—François de la Rochefoucauld

SPEAK YOUR PEAS

"I don't like spinach, and I'm glad I don't, because if I liked it I'd eat it, and I just hate it."

—Clarence Darrow

"The beet is the most intense of vegetables. The radish, admittedly, is more feverish, but the fire of the radish is a cold fire, the fire of discontent, not of passion. Tomatoes are lusty enough, yet there runs through tomatoes an undercurrent of frivolity. Beets are deadly serious."

—Tom Robbins

"Most plants taste better when they've had to suffer a little."

—Diana Kennedy

"It's difficult to think anything but pleasant thoughts while eating a homegrown tomato."

—Lewis Grizzard

"Wild carrots belong to Mercury, and expel wind and remove stitches in the side, promote the flow of urine and women's courses, and break and expel the stone; the seed has the same effect and is good for dropsy, and those whose bowels are swollen with wind."

—Nicholas Culpeper

"I am thinking of the onion again…Not self-righteous like the proletarian potato, nor a siren like the apple. No show-off like the banana. But a modest, self-effacing vegetable, questioning, introspective, peeling itself away, or merely radiating halos like ripples."

—Erica Jong

> In the water bucket
> a melon and an eggplant
> nodding to each other

—Yosa Buson

CHAPTER 9

ON CABBAGE

"CABBAGE: a vegetable about as large and wise as a man's head."

—Ambrose Bierce

"Having a good wife and rich cabbage soup, seek not other things."

—Russian proverb

"The cabbage surpasses all other vegetables. If, at a banquet, you wish to dine a lot and enjoy your dinner, then eat as much cabbage as you wish, seasoned with vinegar, before dinner, and likewise after dinner eat some half-dozen leaves. It will make you feel as if you had not eaten, and you can drink as much as you like."

—Cato

"A garden, though, is a finite place, in which a gardener (or several gardeners) has created, working with or against nature, a plot whose intention it is to provide pleasure; possibly in the form of beauty, possibly in the form of cabbages—and possibly, beautiful cabbages."

—Abby Adams

"It's no use boiling your cabbage twice."

—Irish proverb

"Cabbage as a food has problems. It is easy to grow, a useful source of greenery for much of the year. Yet as a vegetable it has original sin, and needs improvement. It can smell foul in the pot, linger through the house with pertinacity, and ruin a meal with its wet flab. Cabbage also has a nasty history of being good for you."

—Jane Grigson

"In the night the cabbages catch at the moon, the leaves drip silver, the rows of cabbages are a series of little silver waterfalls in the moon."

—Carl Sandburg

"I want death to find me planting my cabbage."

—Michel de Montaigne

HMMM...

"Gentle Reader, The Word will leap on you with leopard man iron claws, it will cut off fingers and toes like an opportunity land crab, it will coil round your thighs like a bushmaster and inject a shot glass of rancid ectoplasm."

—William S. Burroughs

THE CAT IN THE QUOTE COMES BACK

"A cat is a puzzle for which there is no solution."

—Hazel Nicholson

"There are two means of refuge from the miseries of life: music and cats."

—Albert Schweitzer

"If I die before my cat, I want a little of my ashes put in his food so I can live inside him."

—Drew Barrymore

"Nature abhors a vacuum, but not as much as cats do."

—Nelson A. Crawford

"If you hold a cat by the tail you learn things you cannot learn any other way."

—Mark Twain

"To err is human, to purr feline."

—Robert Byrne

TICK...TICK...TICK...

"Tobacco, coffee, alcohol, hashish, prussic acid, strychnine are weak dilutions; the surest poison is time."

—Ralph Waldo Emerson

"But what minutes! Count them by sensation, and not by calendars, and each moment is a day."

—Benjamin Disraeli

"At my back I often hear Time's winged chariot changing gear."

—Eric Linklater

"Time would become meaningless if there were too much of it."

—Ray Kurzweil

"Clocks slay time...time is dead as long as it is being clicked off by little wheels; only when the clock stops does time come to life."

—William Faulkner

"Time is the only critic without ambition."

—John Steinbeck

"An unhurried sense of time is in itself a form of wealth."

—Bonnie Friedman

"Time is an illusion. Lunchtime doubly so."

—Douglas Adams

HE WHO LAUGHS

"He who laughs last laughs best."

—Anonymous

"He who laughs last didn't get it."

—Helen Giangregorio

"He who laughs, lasts."

—Mary Poole

"He who lasts laughs."

—Anonymous

"He who laughs has not yet heard the bad news."

—Bertolt Brecht

IF AT FIRST...

"If at first you don't succeed, your skydiving days are over."

—Milton Berle

"If at first you don't succeed, find out if the loser gets anything."

—Bill Lyon

"If at first you don't succeed, before you try again, stop to figure out what you did wrong."

—Leo Rosten

"If at first you don't succeed, failure may be your style."

—Quentin Crisp

"If at first you don't succeed, let the search engine try."

—Anonymous

"If at first you don't succeed, try, try, and try again. Then give up. There's no use being a damned fool about it."

—W. C. Fields

THE INGREDIENTS OF HAPPINESS

"One is happy as a result of one's own efforts, once one knows the necessary ingredients of happiness—simple tastes, a certain degree of courage, self-denial to a point, love of work, and above all, a clear conscience."

—George Sand

OLD-TIME COMEDY

"I told the doctor I broke my leg in two places. He told me to quit going to those places."

—Henny Youngman

"My brother is very superstitious. He won't work any week that has a Friday in it."

—Milton Berle

"What I don't like about office Christmas parties is looking for a job the next day."

—Phyllis Diller

"Give me golf clubs, fresh air, and a beautiful partner, and you can keep the clubs and the fresh air."

—Jack Benny

"Health nuts are going to feel stupid someday, lying in hospitals dying of nothing."

—Redd Foxx

"I read a book twice as fast as anybody else. First, I read the beginning, and then I read the ending, and then I start in the middle and read toward whatever end I like best."

—Gracie Allen

"The Steinway people have asked me to announce that this is a Baldwin piano."

—Victor Borge

"For the amateur, the funniest thing in the world is the sight of a man dressed up as an old woman rolling down a steep hill in a wheelchair and crashing into a wall at the bottom of it. But to make a pro laugh, it would have to be a *real* old woman.

—Groucho Marx

NOT SO DUMB

"If the Aborigine drafted an I.Q. test, all of Western civilization would presumably flunk it."

—Stanley Garn

"I'm not dumb. I just have a command of thoroughly useless information."

—Bill Watterson

"They say that the more a person learns, the more they find there is to learn. Therefore the smarter you think you are, the dumber you really are."

—Chris Hamono

"Nowadays it is about as big a crime to be dumb as it is to be dishonest."

—Will Rogers

"The dumber people think you are, the more surprised they're going to be when you kill them."

—William Clayton

"Think about how stupid the average person is, then realize that half the population is stupider."

—**George Carlin**

THAT SMARTS

"In the republic of mediocrity, genius is dangerous."

—**Robert G. Ingersoll**

"'Tis not knowing much, but what is useful, that makes a wise man."

—**Thomas Fuller**

"Since when was genius found respectable?"

—**Elizabeth Barrett Browning**

"Everyone is born a genius, but the process of living de-geniuses them."

—**R. Buckminster Fuller**

"The brain is a wonderful organ. It starts working the moment you get up in the morning and does not stop until you get into the office."

—**Robert Frost**

"Ignorance is no excuse—it's the real thing."

—**Jean Kerr**

"Some folks are wise, and some are otherwise."

—**Thomas Smollett**

AGE BEFORE USING

"I have enjoyed greatly the second blooming that comes when you finish the life of the emotions and of personal relations; and suddenly find—at the age of fifty, say—that a whole new life has opened before you, filled with things you can think about, study, or read about…It is as if a fresh sap of ideas and thoughts was rising in you."

—Agatha Christie

SMART MOUTH: ROBIN WILLIAMS

"Beer commercials usually have big men, manly men doing manly things. 'You just killed a small animal. It's time for a light beer.' Why not a realistic beer commercial like, 'It's five o'clock in the morning. You just pissed on a dumpster. It's Miller time.'"

"Canada's like a loft apartment over a really great party."

"Why'd she get her tongue pierced? She said, 'To enhanthe the thekthual thimulathon.'"

"Politics: 'Poli,' a Latin word meaning 'many'; and 'tics,' meaning 'bloodsucking creatures'."

"These people are so rich they don't get crabs…they get lobsters."

"Cricket is basically baseball on valium."

"I've got the fifth sense: I *smell* dead people."

THE OLD DAYS

And none will hear the postman's knock
Without a quickening of the heart.
For who can bear to feel himself forgotten?

—W. H. Auden

MORE THOUGHTS ON
THE HUMAN CONDITION

"The art of living is more like wrestling than dancing."

—Marcus Aurelius

"Life is the art of drawing without an eraser."

—John Gardner

"Life is like a game of cards. The hand that is dealt you is determinism; the way you play it is free will."

—Jawaharlal Nehru

"There is only one basic human right: the right to do as you damn well please. And with it comes the only basic human duty, the duty to take the consequences."

—P. J. O'Rourke

"Life is like a B-picture script. It's that corny. If I had my life story offered to me to film, I'd turn it down."

—Kirk Douglas

"Life is a game show where the people who enjoy it are the winners."

—Orson Bean

"Life is uncertain. Eat dessert first."

—**Ernestine Ulmer**

GOOD TO THE LAST DROP

"I am learning all the time. The tombstone will be my diploma."

—**Eartha Kitt**

GOOD THINKING

"Well done is better than well said."

—**Benjamin Franklin**

"I don't want to live—I want to love first, and live incidentally."

—**Zelda Fitzgerald**

"It's never too late—in fiction or in life—to revise."

—**Nancy Thayer**

"Weak minds sink under prosperity as well as adversity; but strong and deep ones have two high tides."

—**David Hare**

"There is only one thing more powerful than all the armies of the world, and that is an idea whose time has come."

—**Victor Hugo**

"Nothing in life is to be feared. It is only to be understood."

—**Marie Curie**

"Men of genius are not quick judges of character. Deep thinking and high imagining blunt that trivial instinct by which you and I size people up."

—Max Beerbohm

"Every great mistake has a halfway moment, a split second when it can be recalled and perhaps remedied."

—Pearl S. Buck

"Courage does not always roar. Sometimes it is the quiet voice at the day, saying, 'I will try again tomorrow'."

—Anonymous

DON'T!

"Don't speak unless you can improve on the silence."

—Spanish proverb

"Don't worry about people stealing an idea. If it's original, you will have to ram it down their throats."

—Howard Aiken

"Don't sleep too much. If you sleep three hours less each night for a year, you will have an extra month and a half to succeed in."

—Aristotle Onassis

"Don't think there are no crocodiles because the water is calm."

—Malayan proverb

"Don't try to live forever. You will not succeed."

—George Bernard Shaw

"Don't accept your dog's admiration as conclusive evidence that you are wonderful."

—Ann Landers

SATURDAY NIGHT QUOTES

"This week General Electric announced a recall of 3.1 million dishwashers. After hearing that there are over three million dishwashers in the United States, Pat Buchanan called once again for stricter immigration laws."

—Colin Quinn

"Blimpie has started supplying subs for Delta Airlines to serve on its flights. And, in return, Delta is giving Blimpies barf bags to hand out in its restaurants."

—Norm MacDonald

"Retired Army General William C. Westmoreland stated this week that the advances made in medicine as a result of the Vietnam War have saved more lives than those lost in that conflict. Accordingly, the Pentagon has recommended that the United States immediately begin World War III in the hope of wiping out all disease."

—Bill Murray

"California voters rejected all four of Governor Arnold Schwarzenegger's ballot proposals, all of them, every one, including Number One: No hogging the bench press. Number Two: Towel off the incline board. Number Three: Put the free weights back on the rack after use. And Number Four: Let me squeeze your buttocks and don't tell nobody."

—Tina Fey

ON SUPERSTITION

"Superstition, idolatry, and hypocrisy have ample wages, but truth goes begging."

—Martin Luther

"Superstition is to religion what astrology is to astronomy: the mad daughter of a wise mother."

—Voltaire

"The root of all superstition is that men observe when a thing hits, but not when it misses."

—Francis Bacon

"Superstition, bigotry, and prejudice, ghosts though they are, cling tenaciously to life; they are shades armed with tooth and claw. They must be grappled with unceasingly, for it is a fateful part of human destiny that it is condemned to wage perpetual war against ghosts. A shade is not easily taken by the throat and destroyed."

—Victor Hugo

"I have an irrational fear of antique furniture, and I won't get on a plane if the last word I hear ends in 'th' or 'd,' because death ends in 'th', and dead ends in 'd'. Like, if you say to me, 'Have a nice trip, say hello to Fred,' I'll make you say something else."

—Billy Bob Thornton

"I have only one superstition. I make sure I touch all bases when I hit a home run."

—Babe Ruth

SMART MOUTH: JOHN STEINBECK

"I have never smuggled anything in my life. Why, then, do I feel an uneasy sense of guilt on approaching a customs barrier?"

"I've seen a look in dogs' eyes, a quickly vanishing look of amazed contempt, and I am convinced that basically dogs think humans are nuts."

"It would be absurd if we did not understand both angels and devils, since we invented them."

"Man, unlike any other thing organic or inorganic in the universe, grows beyond his work, walks up the stairs of his concepts, emerges ahead of his accomplishments."

"No man really knows about other human beings. The best he can do is to suppose that they are like himself."

"It is a common experience that a problem difficult at night is resolved in the morning after the committee of sleep has worked on it."

"We spend our time searching for security and hate it when we get it."

"Men do change, and change comes like a little wind that ruffles the curtains at dawn, and it comes like the stealthy perfume of wildflowers hidden in the grass."

"If you're in trouble, or hurt or in need—go to the poor people. They're the only ones that'll help—the only ones."

"I am impelled, not to squeak like a grateful and apologetic mouse, but to roar like a lion out of pride in my profession."

"I hate cameras. They are so much more sure than I am about everything."

THAT'S FATE

"Most gods throw dice, but Fate plays chess, and you don't find out till too late that he's been playing with two queens all along."

—Terry Pratchett

CHAPTER 10

FLOWER FACES

"Flowers have an expression of countenance as much as men or animals. Some seem to smile; some have a sad expression; some are pensive and diffident; others again are plain, honest and upright, like the broad-faced sunflower and the hollyhock."

—Henry Ward Beecher

LIFE, DEATH AND A GIRAFFE FILLED WITH WHIPPED CREAM

"Life is better than death, I believe, if only because it is less boring, and because it has fresh peaches in it."

—Alice Walker

"Ignore death up to the last moment; then, when it can't be ignored any longer, have yourself squirted full of morphine and shuffle off in a coma. Thoroughly sensible, humane, and scientific, eh?"

—Aldous Huxley

"You can't always write a chord ugly enough to say what you want to say, so sometimes you have to rely on a giraffe filled with whipped cream."

—Frank Zappa

WIDE WORLD OF PROVERBS

"A broken hand works, but not a broken heart."

—Iran

"A tree falls the way it leans."

—Bulgaria

"Insults should be written in sand, compliments carved in stone."

—Saudi Arabia

"A wise man hears one word and understands two."

—Yiddish

"If you wish to die young, make your physician your heir."

—Romania

"A friend's eye is a good mirror."

—Ireland

"He that falls by himself never cries."

—Turkey

"There is no god like one's stomach; we must sacrifice to it every day."

—Benin

"He who strikes first, strikes twice."

—Mexico

"Luck is loaned, not owned."

—Norway

ONE FOR THE MONEY

"A dollar picked up in the road is more satisfaction to us than the ninety-nine which we had to work for, and the money won at Faro or in the stock market snuggles into our hearts in the same way."

—Mark Twain

TWO FOR THE SHOW

"Show business is and has always been a depraved carnival."

—David Mamet

"There's no doubt about it, show business lures the people who didn't get enough love, attention, or approval early in life and have grown up to become bottomless, gaping vessels of terrifying, abject need. Please laugh."

—Dennis Miller

THREE TO GET READY

"Before everything else, getting ready is the secret of success."

—Henry Ford

"We are always getting ready to live, but never living."

—Ralph Waldo Emerson

"I could just remember how my father used to say that the reason for living was to get ready to stay dead a long time."

—William Faulkner

FOUR TO GO

"When the going gets tough, the tough get going."

—Joseph P. Kennedy

"Wherever you go, go with all your heart."

—Confucius

"If you are going through hell, keep going."

—Winston Churchill

> Let my people go-go-go
> Let my people go-go-go
> Let my people go-go-go
> Let my people go

—The Rainmakers, "Let My People Go-Go"

ON FORGIVENESS

"'I can forgive, but I cannot forget,' is only another way of saying 'I will not forgive.' Forgiveness ought to be like a canceled note torn in two and burned up, so that it never can be shown against one."

—Henry Ward Beecher

SMART MOUTH: ROGER EBERT

"*Dirty Love* wasn't written and directed, it was committed. Here is a film so pitiful, it doesn't rise to the level of badness. It is hopelessly incompetent...I am not certain that anyone involved has ever seen a movie, or knows what one is."

"I had a colonoscopy once, and they let me watch it on TV. It was more entertaining than *The Brown Bunny*."

"*Gone in 60 Seconds* is the kind of movie that ends up playing on the TV set over the bar in a better movie."

"*Mr. Magoo* is a one-joke movie without the joke."

"*Mad Dog Time* is the first movie I have seen that does not improve on the sight of a blank screen viewed for the same length of time."

"Yes, I take notes during the movies. During a movie like *House of D*, I jot down words I think might be useful in the review. Peering now at my three-by-five cards, I read 'sappy,' 'inane,' 'cornball,' 'shameless,' and, my favorite, 'doofusoid.' I sigh. This film has not even inspired interesting adjectives, except for the one I made up myself."

"I think the future of the republic may depend on young audiences seeing more movies like *Whale Rider* and fewer movies like *Scooby-Doo 2*, but then that's just me."

TOUCHÉ!

"A diplomat...is a person who can tell you to go to hell in such a way that you actually look forward to the trip."

—Caskie Stinnett

"A real diplomat is one who can cut his neighbor's throat without having his neighbor notice it."

—Trygve Lie

"Diplomacy is the art of saying 'Nice doggie' until you can find a rock."

—Will Rogers

"To say nothing, especially when speaking, is half the art of diplomacy."

—Will Durant

SHUTTER TO THINK

"A great photograph is a full expression of what one feels about what is being photographed in the deepest sense, and is, thereby, a true expression of what one feels about life in its entirety."

—Ansel Adams

"I didn't want to tell the tree or weed what it was. I wanted it to tell me something and through me express its meaning in nature."

—Wynn Bullock

"It's weird that photographers spend years or even a whole lifetime trying to capture moments that added together, don't even amount to a couple of hours."

—James Lalropui Keivom

"Actually, I'm not all that interested in the subject of photography. Once the picture is in the box, I'm not all that interested in what happens next. Hunters, after all, aren't cooks."

—Henri Cartier-Bresson

"Perishability in a photograph is important in a picture. If a photograph looks perishable we say, 'Gee, I'm glad I have that moment.'"

—John Loengard

THE WIN/LOSS COLUMN

"Win as if you were used to it, lose as if you enjoyed it for a change."

—Ralph Waldo Emerson

"There is nothing to winning, really. That is, if you happen to be blessed with a keen eye, an agile mind, and no scruples whatsoever."

—Alfred Hitchcock

"Those that know how to win are much more numerous than those who know how to make proper use of their victories."

—Polybius

"I never did say that you can't be a nice guy and win. I said that if I was playing third base and my mother rounded third with the winning run, I'd trip her up."

—Leo Durocher

"No one wants to quit when he's losing and no one wants to quit when he's winning."

—Richard Strauss

"Conquer, but don't triumph."

—Marie von Ebner-Eschenbach

"If winning isn't everything, why do they keep score?"

—Vince Lombardi

LET'S TALK, AGAIN

"Speak when you are angry—and you'll make the best speech you'll ever regret."

—Laurence J. Peter

"Speech was given to man to disguise his thoughts."

—Charles M. de Talleyrand

"Make sure you have finished speaking before your audience has finished listening."

—Dorothy Sarnoff

"When at a loss how to go on, in speaking, cough."

—Greek proverb

"Let your speech be always with grace, seasoned with salt, that ye may know how ye ought to answer every man."

—Colossians 4:6

"For mankind, speech with a capital S is especially meaningful and committing, more than the content communicated. The outcry of the newborn and the sound of the bells are fraught with mystery more than the baby's woeful face or the venerable tower."

—Paul Goodman

HELPING HANDS

"Many will show you the way once your cart has overturned."

—Turkish proverb

WRITE THIS DOWN

"A professional writer is an amateur who didn't quit."

—Richard Bach

SMART MOUTH: PABLO PICASSO

"God is really only another artist. He invented the giraffe, the elephant, and the cat. He has no real style, he just goes on trying other things."

"Painting is a blind man's profession. He paints not what he sees, but what he feels, what he tells himself about what he has seen."

"As a child I could draw like Leonardo, as an adult I want to paint as a child."

"I hate that aesthetic game of the eye and the mind, played by these connoisseurs, these mandarins who 'appreciate' beauty. What is beauty, anyway? There's no such thing. I never 'appreciate,' any more than I 'like.' I love or I hate."

"To finish a picture? What nonsense! To finish it means to be through with it, to kill it, to rid it of its soul, to give it its final blow."

"We artists are indestructible; even in a prison, or in a concentration camp, I would be almighty in my own world of art, even if I had to paint my pictures with my wet tongue on the dusty floor of my cell."

"If there were only one truth, you couldn't paint a hundred canvases on the same theme."

THE NAKED TRUTH

"I am sure no other civilization, not even the Romans, has showed such a vast proportion of ignominious and degraded nudity, and ugly, squalid, dirty sex. Because no other civilization has driven sex into the underworld, and nudity to the W.C."

—D. H. Lawrence, on British civilization

"Full nakedness! All my joys are due to thee, as souls unbodied, bodies unclothed must be, to taste whole joys."

—John Donne

"When you've seen a nude infant doing a backward somersault, you know why clothing exists."

—Stephen Fry

"Nakedness reveals itself. Nudity is placed on display. The nude is condemned to never being naked. Nudity is a form of dress."

—John Berger

"Beware of the naked man who offers you his shirt."

—Navjot Singh Sidhu

"I'd like to see a nude opera, because when they hit those high notes, I bet you can really see it in those genitals."

—Jack Handey

A DEEP THOUGHT

I to the world am like a drop of water
That in the ocean seeks another drop,
Who, falling there to find his fellow forth,
Unseen, inquisitive, confounds himself.

—William Shakespeare

A STEEP THOUGHT

"Remember when life's path is steep to keep your mind even."

—Horace

IT'S A CONSPIRACY...OR NOT

"In politics, nothing happens by accident. If it happened, you can bet it was planned that way."

—Franklin Delano Roosevelt

"More things in politics happen by accident or exhaustion than happen by conspiracy."

—Jeff Greenfield

"The world is governed by people far different from those imagined by the public."

—Benjamin Disraeli

"Anyone who knows how difficult it is to keep a secret among three men—particularly if they are married—knows how absurd is the idea of a worldwide secret conspiracy consciously controlling all mankind by its financial power; in real, clear analysis."

—Oswald Mosley

"The biggest conspiracy has always been the fact that there is no conspiracy. Nobody's out to get you. Nobody gives a sh*t whether you live or die. There, you feel better now?"

—Dennis Miller

ONE FOR YOU...

"I do not want a friend who smiles when I smile, who weeps when I weep; for my shadow in the pool can do better than that."

—Confucius

...AND ONE FOR ME

"I dote on myself, there is that lot of me and all so luscious."

—Walt Whitman

JUSTICE

"I have always found that mercy bears richer fruits than strict justice."

—Abraham Lincoln

"It is necessary for him who lays out a state and arranges laws for it to presuppose that all men are evil and that they are always going to act according to the wickedness of their spirits whenever they have free scope."
—Niccolò Machiavelli

"The law must be stable, but it must not stand still."
—Roscoe Pound

"At his best, man is the noblest of all animals. Separated from law and justice, he is the worst."
—Aristotle

"Justice limps along...but it gets there all the same."
—Gabriel García Márquez

GOOD ADVICE

"There are times not to flirt. When you're sick. When you're with children. When you're on the witness stand."
—Joyce Jillson

TROUBLE, TROUBLE SET ME FREE...

"What to do if you find yourself stuck in a crack in the ground underneath a giant boulder you can't move, with no hope of rescue. Consider how lucky you are that life has been good to you so far. Alternatively, if life hasn't been good to you so far, which given your current circumstances seems more likely, consider how lucky you are that it won't be troubling you much longer."
—Douglas Adams

WORM

"This transformation in kids—from flashing dragonflies, so to say, to sticky water-surface worms slowly slipping downstream—is noticed with pride by society and with mortification by God."

—William Saroyan

"Life is hard. Then you die. Then they throw dirt in your face. Then the worms eat you. Be grateful it happens in that order."

—David Gerrold

"Man cannot make a worm, yet he will make gods by the dozen"

—Michel de Montaigne

O Rose, thou art sick!
The invisible worm,
That flies in the night,
In the howling storm,
Has found out thy bed
Of crimson joy;
And his dark secret love
Does thy life destroy.

—William Blake

A GURU'S VIEW

"Life and death come to all who are born. Everything here gets devoured by Death. He sits and examines the accounts, there where no one goes along with anyone. Those who weep and wail might just as well all tie bundles of straw."

—Sri Guru Granth Sahib

FIRST FISH STORY

"Fiction was invented the day Jonas arrived home and told his wife that he was three days late because he had been swallowed by a whale."

—Gabriel García Márquez

OH, MAMA

"My mother could make anybody feel guilty—she used to get letters of apology from people she didn't even know."

—Joan Rivers

"A mother is not a person to lean on, but a person to make leaning unnecessary."

—Dorothy Canfield Fisher

"Before becoming a mother, I had a hundred theories on how to bring up children. Now I have seven children and only one theory: Love them, especially when they least deserve to be loved."

—Kate Samperi

"A suburban mother's role is to deliver children obstetrically once, and by car forever after."

—Peter De Vries

"When you are a mother, you are never really alone in your thoughts. A mother always has to think twice, once for herself and once for her child."

—Sophia Loren

"No matter how old a mother is, she watches her middle-aged children for signs of improvement."
—Florida Scott-Maxwell

"Mothers are fonder than fathers of their children because they are more certain they are their own."
—Aristotle

"Blaming mother is just a negative way of clinging to her still."
—Nancy Friday

"The story of a mother's life: Trapped between a scream and a hug."
—Cathy Guisewite

A GRAVE THOUGHT

"There are so many little dyings, it doesn't matter which of them is death."
—Kenneth Patchen

HEAD, SHOULDERS, KNEES AND TOES...

"How beautiful are thy feet with shoes, O prince's daughter! the joints of thy thighs are like jewels, the work of the hands of a cunning workman."
—Song of Songs

"Ankles are nearly always neat and good-looking, but knees are nearly always not."
—Dwight D. Eisenhower

"The legs are the wheels of creativity."

—Albert Einstein

"Speak in French when you can't think of English for a thing—turn out your toes when you walk—and remember who you are!"

—Lewis Carroll

"Although the whole mind seems to be united to the whole body, I recognize that if a foot or arm is cut off, nothing has thereby been taken away from the mind."

—René Descartes

"I often think that a slightly exposed shoulder emerging from a long satin nightgown packed more sex than two naked bodies in bed."

—Bette Davis

"Your body is not the real you, it's just the meat you live in. I like that: it means that the real me doesn't really have a humongous butt."

—Jessica Zafra

"If you ever need a helping hand, you'll find one at the end of your arm."

—Yiddish proverb

"When a finger points to the moon, the imbecile looks at the finger."

—Chinese proverb

SMART MOUTH: TRUMAN CAPOTE

"Well, I'm about as tall as a shotgun, and just as noisy."

"The truth seems to be that no one likes to see himself described as he is. Well, even I can understand that—because I don't like it myself when I am the sitter and not the portraitist: the frailty of egos! —and the more accurate the strokes, the greater the resentment."

"Style makes the middle class nervous."

"I'm not a saint yet. I'm an alcoholic. I'm a drug addict. I'm homosexual. I'm a genius. Of course I could be all four of these dubious things and still be a saint. But I ain't."

"People who are having a love-sex relationship are continuously lying to each other because the very nature of the relationship demands that they do, because you have to make a love object of this person, which means that you editorialize about them. You cut out what you don't want to see, you add this if it isn't there. And so therefore you're building a lie."

"I love elegant women. They're like art and music. But I want them all to look as if they were living private lives. Not as if they were going onstage about to do the tarantella."

GRACEFUL ENDING

"In life as in dance: Grace glides on blistered feet."

—Alice Abrams

CHAPTER 11

SOMETHING TO THINK ABOUT

"My God! The English language is a form of communication! Conversation isn't just crossfire where you shoot and get shot at! Where you've got to duck for your life and aim to kill! Words aren't only bombs and bullets—no, they're little gifts, containing meanings!"

—Philip Roth

I DO

"Nearly all marriages, even happy ones, are mistakes: in the sense that almost certainly both partners might be found more suitable mates. But the real soul-mate is the one you are actually married to."

—J. R. R. Tolkien

"Marriage is a lottery, but you can't tear up your ticket if you lose."

—F. M. Knowles

"The world has suffered more from the ravages of ill-advised marriages than from virginity."

—Ambrose Bierce

"If I get married again, I want a guy there with a drum to do rim-shots during the vows."

—Sam Kinison

"I first learned the concepts of nonviolence in my marriage."

—Mohandas K. Gandhi

CRACKED

"Those prizes in Cracker Jacks are a joke. I once got a magnifying glass. It was so poorly made, ants were laughing at it."

—Scott Roeben

SMART MOUTH: BENJAMIN "POOR RICHARD" FRANKLIN

"A rich rogue is like a fat hog, who never does good 'til as dead as a log."

"Take this remark from Richard poor and lame, whate'er's begun in anger ends in shame."

"He that lives on hope will die fasting."

"Don't think to hunt two hares with one dog."

"He that waits upon fortune is never sure of a dinner."

"When you speak to a man, look on his eyes; when he speaks to thee, look on his mouth."

"You may delay, but time will not."

"Let thy discontents be thy secrets; if the world knows them, it will despise thee and increase them."

"He that best understands the world, least likes it."

"None are deceived, but they that confide."

"Death takes no bribes."

HMMM...

"Sometimes I like to pretend that I'm deaf, and try to imagine what it's like not to be able to hear the birds. It's not that bad."

—Larry David

FROM THE LABORATORY, PART TWO

"Whenever science makes a discovery, the devil grabs it while the angels are debating the best way to use it."

—Alan Valentine

"Most institutions demand unqualified faith; but the institution of science makes skepticism a virtue."

—Robert K. Merton

"The greatest discoveries of science have always been those that forced us to rethink our beliefs about the universe and our place in it."

—Robert L. Park

"It requires a very unusual mind to undertake the analysis of the obvious."

—Alfred North Whitehead

"And who can doubt that it will lead to the worst disorders when minds created free by God are compelled to submit slavishly to an outside will? When we are told to deny our senses and subject them to the whim of others? When people devoid of whatsoever competence are made judges over experts and are granted authority to treat them as they please? These are the novelties which are apt to bring about the ruin of commonwealths and the subversion of the state."

—Galileo Galilei

"True science teaches, above all, to doubt and be ignorant."

—Miguel de Unamuno

"All of us are guinea pigs in the laboratory of God. Humanity is just a work in progress."

—Tennessee Williams

DEEP NOSE THOUGHT

"Love is like a booger. You keep picking at it until you get it, then wonder what to do with it."

—Anonymous

DEEP EAR THOUGHT

"'What's your secret?' my friend asks me. 'Probably that I steal people's pets and then return them for the reward money,' I reply. 'No,' he says. 'I mean, what's the secret to your easygoing, worry-free, almost criminally naive outlook on life?' 'Oh, that's easy,' I tell him. 'Every January, I get the wax professionally removed from my ears.'"

—**Mark Bazar**

MORE DEADLY WEAPUNS

"If you want to see a comic strip, you should see me in the shower."

—**Groucho Marx**

"The antiques my wife buys at auctions are keeping me baroque."

—**Peter De Vries**

"Putting your hands in the earth is very grounding."

—**John Glover**

"The Passion of the Christ opened up on Ash Wednesday, and had a Good Friday."

—**Billy Crystal**

"An art thief is a man who takes pictures."

—**George Carlin**

"A jester unemployed is nobody's fool!"

—**Danny Kaye**

"A bore is a person who opens his mouth and puts his feats in it."
—**Henry Ford**

"I'd call him a sadistic, hippophilic necrophile, but that would be beating a dead horse."
—**Woody Allen**

RANDOM BITS OF WISDOM

"Education is when you read the fine print; experience is what you get when you don't."
—**Pete Seeger**

"If only we'd stop trying to be happy we'd have a pretty good time."
—**Edith Wharton**

"He who cannot obey himself will be commanded. That is the nature of living creatures."
—**Friedrich Nietzsche**

"The doctor sees all the weakness of mankind, the lawyer all the wickedness, the theologian all the stupidity."
—**Arthur Schopenhauer**

"Growth itself contains the germ of happiness."
—**Pearl S. Buck**

"Wisdom is knowing what to do next, skill is knowing how to do it, and virtue is doing it."
—**David Starr Jordan**

"I love quotations because it is a joy to find thoughts one might have, beautifully expressed with much authority by someone recognizably wiser than oneself."

—Marlele Dietrich

"Time ripens all things, no man is born wise."

—Miguel de Cervantes

DRAGON SLAYERS

"Fairy tales are more than true; not because they tell us that dragons exist, but because they tell us that dragons can be beaten."

—G. K. Chesterton

THE TRUTH (ABOUT THE TRUTH)

"In an age of universal deceit, telling the truth is a revolutionary act."

—George Orwell

"The third time you say a thing, it sounds like a lie."

—Harrison Ford

"A fact will fit every other fact in the universe, and that is how you can tell whether it is or is not a fact. A lie will not fit anything except another lie."

—Robert G. Ingersoll

"Truth, like light, blinds. Falsehood, on the contrary, is a beautiful twilight that enhances every object."

—Albert Camus

"Chase after the truth like all hell and you'll free yourself, even though you never touch its coattails."

—Clarence Darrow

"You shall know the truth, and the truth shall make you mad as hell."

—Aldous Huxley

NAME THAT QUOTE

"The name of a man is a numbing blow from which he never recovers."

—Marshall McLuhan

"I've made up so many stories about my where my name comes from, I can't remember."

—Joaquin Phoenix

"Proper names are poetry in the raw. Like all poetry they are untranslatable."

—W. H. Auden

"I've always thought that a name says a lot about a person. So naturally, being named Howard, I always wanted to crawl into a hole."

—Howard Stern

"Nicknames stick to people, and the most ridiculous are the most adhesive."

—Thomas C. Haliburton

"I confused things with their names: that is belief."

—Jean-Paul Sartre

"Tigers die and leave their skins; people die and leave their names."

—Japanese proverb

WHO, WHAT, WHERE, WHEN...

"When you were born, you cried and the world rejoiced. Live your life so that when you die, the world cries and you rejoice."

—Anonymous

Forward, the Light Brigade!
Was there a man dismay'd?
Not tho' the soldier knew
Someone had blunder'd:
Theirs not to make reply,
Theirs not to reason why,
Theirs but to do and die:
Into the valley of Death
Rode the six hundred.

—Alfred, Lord Tennyson

"You must constantly ask yourself these questions: Who am I around? What are they doing to me? What have they got me reading? What have they got me saying? Where do they have me going? What do they have me thinking? And most important, what do they have me becoming? Then ask yourself the big question: Is that okay? Your life does not get better by chance, it gets better by change."

—Jim Rohn

"If you don't know where you are going, you will probably end up somewhere else."

—**Laurence J. Peter**

I keep six honest serving men
(They taught me all I knew)
Their names are What and Why and When
And How and Where and Who.

—**Rudyard Kipling**

HMMM...

"If there are no stupid questions, then what kind of questions do stupid people ask? Do they get smart just in time to ask questions?"

—**Scott Adams**

THOUGHT BALLOONS

"Cartoonist was the weirdest name I finally let myself have. I would never say it. When I heard it I silently thought, what an awful word."

—**Lynda Barry**

"Today you are You, that is truer than true. There is no one alive who is Youer than You."

—**Dr. Seuss**

"I will go to my grave in a state of abject endless fascination that we all have the capacity to become emotionally involved with a personality that doesn't exist."

—**Berkeley Breathed**

"Nothing defines humans better than their willingness to do irrational things in the pursuit of phenomenally unlikely pay-offs. This is the principle behind lotteries, dating, and religion."

—Scott Adams

"God put me on this earth to accomplish a certain number of things. Right now I am so far behind that I will never die."

—Bill Watterson

"If you don't like my opinion of you, you can always improve."

—Ashleigh Brilliant

"A lot of people mistake a short memory for a clear conscience."

—Doug Larsen

"The boredom occasioned by too much restraint is always preferable to that produced by an uncontrolled enthusiasm for a pointless variety."

—Osbert Lancaster

"At sixteen I was stupid, confused, and indecisive. At twenty-five I was wise, self-confident, prepossessing, and assertive. At forty-five I am stupid, confused, insecure, and indecisive. Who would have supposed that maturity is only a short break in adolescence?"

—Jules Feiffer

"Life is like a movie. Since there aren't any commercial breaks, you have to get up and go to the bathroom in the middle of it."

—Garry Trudeau

HMMM...

"I love Mickey Mouse more than any woman I have ever known."

—Walt Disney

ON EXTRATERRESTRIALS

"The fancy that extraterrestrial life is by definition of a higher order than our own is one that soothes all children, and many writers."

—Joan Didion

"It was the darnedest thing I've ever seen. It was big, it was very bright, it changed colors, and it was about the size of the moon. We watched it for ten minutes, but none of us could figure out what it was. One thing's for sure, I'll never make fun of people who say they've seen unidentified objects in the sky. If I become president, I'll make every piece of information this country has about UFO sightings available to the public and the scientists."

—Jimmy Carter

"Only man is a narcissistic enough species to think that a highly evolved alien life force would travel across billions and billions of light-years—a group of aliens so intelligent, so insouciant, so utterly above it all, they feel no need whatsoever to equip their spacecraft with windows so that they can gaze out on all that celestial beauty—but then immediately upon landing, their first impulse is to get in some hick's ass with a flashlight."

—Dennis Miller

"Babies have big heads and big eyes, and tiny little bodies with tiny little arms and legs. So did the aliens at Roswell! I rest my case."

—William Shatner

FRANK ADVICE

"Cock your hat—angles are attitudes."

—Frank Sinatra

THAT'S MENTAL

"Some people never go crazy. What truly horrible lives they must lead."

—Charles Bukowski

"Where does the violet tint end and the orange tint begin? Distinctly we see the difference of the colors, but where, exactly, does the one first blending enter into the other? So with sanity and insanity."

—Herman Melville

"Insanity is often the logic of an accurate mind overtaxed."

—Oliver Wendell Holmes

"For me, insanity is super sanity. The normal is psychotic. Normal means lack of imagination, lack of creativity."

—Jean DuBuffet

"A neurosis is a secret that you don't know you are keeping."

—Kenneth Tynan

"A neurotic is a man who builds a castle in the air. A psychotic is the man who lives in it. A psychiatrist is the man who collects the rent."

—Jerome Lawrence

AHEM

"I love to put on lotion. Sometimes I'll watch TV and go into a lotion trance for an hour. I try to find brands that don't taste bad in case anyone wants to taste me."

—Angelina Jolie

TEN TOMS

"Most of the people I admire, they usually smell funny and don't get out much. It's true. Most of them are either dead or not feeling well."

—Tom Waits

"Good things, when short, are twice as good."

—Tom Stoppard

"Things are much more complicated. Feminism versus pornography, for example. There are a lot of feminists who think it is bad, but others think it's good. I have become, you might call it mature—I would call it senile—and I can see both sides. But you can't write a satirical song with 'but on the other hand' in it, or 'however.' It's got to be one-sided."

—Tom Lehrer

"If the highest aim of a captain were to preserve his ship, he would keep it in port forever."

—Thomas Aquinas

"People are born with certain faces, like my father was born with a face people wanted to hit."

—Thom Yorke

"Women are still throwing their undies at me in concert, but now the panties are quite a bit larger than they used to be."

—Tom Jones

"My belief is that 'recluse' is a code word generated by journalists...meaning, 'doesn't like to talk to reporters.'"

—Thomas Pynchon

"Wake love up in the middle of the night. Tell it the world is on fire. Dash to the bedroom window and pee out of it. Casually return to bed and assure love that everything is going to be all right. Fall asleep. Love will be there in the morning."

—Tom Robbins

"Be polite to all, but intimate with few."

—Thomas Jefferson

"Nothing ends nicely, that's why it ends."

—Tom Cruise

WILD KINGDOM

"I go about looking at horses and cattle. They eat grass, make love, work when they have to, bear their young. I am sick with envy of them."

—Sherwood Anderson

"Like the herd animals we are, we sniff warily at the strange one among us."

—Loren Eiseley

"When rats leave a sinking ship, where exactly do they think they're going?"

—**Douglas Gauck**

"I think animal testing is a bad idea; they get all nervous and give the wrong answers."

—**Joseph Blosephina**

"Penguins mate for life. Which doesn't surprise me that much, because they all look alike—it's not like they're gonna meet a better-looking penguin one day."

—**Ellen DeGeneres**

"A man is ethical only when life, as such, is sacred to him, that of plants and animals as that of his fellow men, and when he devotes himself helpfully to all life that is in need of help."

—**Albert Schweitzer**

"Until one has loved an animal, a part of one's soul remains unawakened."

—**Anatole France**

LISTEN

"The deeper the sorrow, the less tongue it has."

—**the Talmud**

CHAPTER 12

VOICE-OVERS

"There is no greater index of character so sure as the voice."

—Benjamin Disraeli

"We often refuse to accept an idea merely because the tone of voice in which it has been expressed is unsympathetic to us."

—Friedrich Nietzsche

"Violence in the voice is often only the death rattle of reason in the throat."

—John F. Boyes

"The voice is nothing but beaten air."

—Seneca

"Then read from the treasured volume the poem of thy choice, and lend to the rhyme of the poet the beauty of thy voice."

—Henry Wadsworth Longfellow

"Screaming is bad for the voice, but it's good for the heart."

—Conor Oberst

"His voice was intimate as the rustle of sheets."

—Dorothy Parker

NAP TIME

"Think what a better world it would be if we all, the whole world, had cookies and milk about three o'clock every afternoon and then lay down on our blankets for a nap."

—Barbara Jordan

"There is more refreshment and stimulation in a nap, even of the briefest, than in all the alcohol ever distilled."

—Ovid

"A nap, my friend, is a brief period of sleep which overtakes superannuated persons when they endeavor to entertain unwelcome visitors or to listen to scientific lectures."

—George Bernard Shaw

"I usually take a two-hour nap from one to four."

—**Yogi Berra**

"No day is so bad it can't be fixed with a nap."

—**Carrie Snow**

EASY, RIDER

And I to my motorcycle
Parked like the soul of the junkyard
Restored, a bicycle fleshed
With power, and tore off
Up Highway 106, continually
Drunk on the wind in my mouth,
Wringing the handlebar for speed,
Wild to be wreckage forever.

—**James Dickey**

COMMON SENSE

"Common sense is the collection of prejudices acquired by age eighteen."

—**Albert Einstein**

"Success is more a function of consistent common sense than it is of genius."

—**An Wang**

"Common sense is the knack of seeing things as they are, and doing things as they ought to be done."

—**C. E. Stowe**

"Common sense is what tells us the earth is flat and the sun goes around it."

—Anonymous

"Common sense and a sense of humor are the same thing, moving at different speeds. A sense of humor is just common sense, dancing."

—William James

"Common sense is the guy that tells you that you ought to have your brakes relined last week before you smashed a front end. Common sense is the Monday-morning quarterback who could have won the ball game if he had been on the team. But he never is. He's high up in the stands with a flask on his hip. Common sense is the little man in the grey suit who never makes a mistake in addition. But it's always someone else's money he's adding up."

—Raymond Chandler

"Common sense is not so common."

—Voltaire

TWO RULES

"Never settle with words what you can accomplish with a flame-thrower."

—Bruce Feirstein

"You may not be able to change the world, but at least you can embarrass the guilty."

—Jessica Mitford

BEARLY THINKING

"When I was a kid my favorite relative was Uncle Caveman. After school we'd all go play in his cave, and every once in a while he would eat one of us. It wasn't until later that I found out that Uncle Caveman was a bear."

—Jack Handey

TIGERLY THINKING

"Do not blame God for having created the tiger, but thank him for not having given it wings."

—Indian proverb

RISING TO IT

"Any concern too small to be turned into a prayer is too small to be made into a burden."

—Corrie ten Boom

"The problem is not that there are problems. The problem is expecting otherwise and thinking that having problems is a problem."

—Theodore Rubin

"What one decides to do in crisis depends on one's philosophy of life, and that philosophy cannot be changed by an incident. If one hasn't any philosophy in crises, others make the decision."

—Jeannette Rankin

"What is to give light must endure burning."

—Viktor Frankl

"Life is thickly sown with thorns, and I know no other remedy than to pass quickly through them. The longer we dwell on our misfortunes, the greater is their power to harm us."

—Voltaire

"Try again. Fail again. Fail better."

—Samuel Beckett

"If the first woman God ever made was strong enough to turn the world upside down, these women together ought to be able to turn it right side up again."

—Sojourner Truth

GOOD ADVICE

"If you have a lot of tension and you get a headache, do what it says on the aspirin bottle: 'Take two aspirin' and 'Keep away from children.'"

—Anonymous

ON JAZZ

"The word 'jazz' in its progress toward respectability has meant first sex, then dancing, then music."

—F. Scott Fitzgerald

"There's more bad music in jazz than any other form. Maybe that's because the audience doesn't really know what's happening."

—Pat Metheny

"Jazz will endure just as long as people hear it through their feet instead of their brains."

—John Philip Sousa

"Jazz is the big brother of the blues. If a guy's playing blues, he's in high school. When he starts playing jazz it's like going on to college, to a school of higher learning."

—B. B. King

"Master your instrument. Master the music. And then forget all that bullsh*t and just play."

—Charlie Parker

"It's like an act of murder. You play with intent to commit something."

—Duke Ellington

"A short jazz poem: Listen!"

—Jon Hendricks

SEX AND THE WITTY, PART TWO

"Sex is like art. Most of it is pretty bad, and the good stuff is out of your price range."

—Scott Roeben

"In America, sex is an obsession. In other parts of the world, it's a fact."

—Marlene Dietrich

"There's people making babies to my music. That's nice."

—Barry White

"Despite a lifetime of service to the cause of sexual liberation, I have never caught venereal disease, which makes me feel rather like an arctic explorer who has never had frostbite."

—Germaine Greer

"Just saying 'no' prevents teenage pregnancy the way 'Have a nice day' cures chronic depression."

—Faye Wattleton

"I'm a terrible lover. I've actually given a woman an anticlimax."

—Scott Roeben

"I'm a great lover, I'll bet."

—Emo Philips

SO TRUE

"The more you observe politics, the more you've got to admit that each party is worse than the other."

—Will Rogers

ON JOURNALISM

"Journalism largely consists of saying 'Lord Jones is dead' to people who never knew Lord Jones was alive."

—G.K. Chesterton

"I call 'journalism' everything that will be less interesting tomorrow than today."

—Andre Gide

"Journalism is the ability to meet the challenge of filling space."

—Rebecca West

"The First Law of Journalism: to confirm existing prejudice, rather than contradict it."

—Alexander Cockburn

"Cronyism is the curse of journalism. After many years I have reached the firm conclusion that it is impossible for any objective newspaperman to be a friend of the president."

—Walter Lippman

"The task of editorial writers is to come down out of the hills after the battle is over and shoot the wounded."

—Murray Kempton

"Journalism is organized gossip."

—Edward Eggleston

"Dealing with the media is more difficult than bathing a leper."

—Mother Teresa

"I don't so much mind that newspapers are dying—it's watching them commit suicide that pisses me off."

—Molly Ivins

"If it's called the *USA Today*, why is all the news from yesterday? BAM. Busted!"

—Stephen Colbert

THE DAILY FISH WRAP

"A 19th century Irish immigrant named O'Reilly called the newspaper a biography of something greater than a man. It is the biography of a DAY. It is a photograph, of twenty-four hours length, of the mysterious river of time that is sweeping past us forever. And yet we take our year's newspapers—which contain more tales of sorrow and suffering, and joy and success, and ambition and defeat, and villainy and virtue, than the greatest book ever written—and we use them to light the fire."

—Adair Lara

OH, BABY

"It is a pleasant thing to reflect upon, and furnishes a complete answer to those who contend for the gradual degeneration of the human species, that every baby born into the world is a finer one than the last."

—Charles Dickens

SEVEN AMERICAN PROVERBS

"After dark, all cats are leopards."

—Zuni

"Don't let yesterday use up too much of today."

—Cherokee

"It is better to have less thunder in the mouth and more lightning in the hand."

—Apache

"A good soldier is a poor scout."

—Cheyenne

"See how the boy is with his sister and you can know how the man will be with your daughter."

—Plains Sioux

"We stand somewhere between the mountain and the ant."

—Onondaga

"All who have died are equal."

—Comanche

GOOD AND EVIL

"The wicked are wicked, no doubt, and they go astray and they fall, and they come by their deserts: but who can tell the mischief which the very virtuous do?"

—William Makepeace Thackeray

"Because everyone knows that good is good, bad exists."

—Lao Tzu

"The line separating good and evil passes not through states, nor between classes, nor between parties either—but right through the human heart."

—Alexandr Solzhenitsyn

"Evil always turns up in this world through some genius or other."

—Denis Diderot

"Somehow our devils are never quite what we expect when we meet them face to face."

—Nelson DeMille

"Good has but one enemy, the evil; but the evil has two enemies, the good and itself."
—Johannes von Müller

"The sad truth is that most evil is done by people who never make up their minds to be good or evil."
—Hannah Arendt

"No one ever became extremely wicked suddenly."
—Juvenal

HUMOR ME

"God writes a lot of comedy. The trouble is, he's stuck with so many bad actors who don't know how to play funny."
—Garrison Keillor

"Comedy is simply a funny way of being serious."
—Peter Ustinov

"Humor is a rubber sword—it allows you to make a point without drawing blood."
—Mary Hirsch

"Comedy is unusual people in real situations; farce is real people in unusual situations."
—Chuck Jones

"Among those whom I like or admire, I can find no common denominator, but among those whom I love, I can: All of them make me laugh."
—W. H. Auden

HMMM...

"Grace, it's Christmas, for goodness' sake. Think about the baby Jesus, up in that tower, letting his hair down, so that the three wise men can climb up and spin the dradel and see if there are six more weeks of winter."

—Karen (Megan Mullally), *Will & Grace*

HYMMMN...

"TEDIUM, n. Ennui, the state or condition of one that is bored. Many fanciful derivations of the word have been affirmed, but so high an authority as Father Jape says that it comes from a very obvious source—the first words of the ancient Latin hymn *Te Deum Laudamus*. In this apparently natural derivation there is something that saddens."

—Ambrose Bierce

MMMM...CHOCOLATE

"Cocoa is the divine drink, which builds up resistance and fights fatigue. A cup of this precious drink permits a man to walk for a whole day without food."

—Montezuma

"There's no metaphysics on Earth like chocolates."

—Fernando Pessoa

"Chocolate makes otherwise normal people melt into strange states of ecstasy."

—John West

"Strength is the capacity to break a chocolate bar into four pieces with your bare hands—and then eat just one of the pieces."

—Judith Viorst

"There is a simple memory aid to determine whether it is the correct time to order chocolate dishes: Any month whose name contains the letter A, E, or U is the proper time for chocolate."

—Sandra Boynton

"Always serve too much hot fudge sauce on hot fudge sundaes. It makes people overjoyed, and puts them in your debt."

—Judith Olney

"My therapist told me the way to achieve true inner peace is to finish what I start. So far today, I have finished two bags of M&Ms and a chocolate cake. I feel better already."

—Dave Barry

GOOD AND EVIL, PART TWO

"I've met God across his long walnut desk with his diplomas hanging on the wall behind him, and God asks me, 'Why? Why did I cause so much pain? Didn't I realize that each of us is a sacred, unique snowflake of special unique specialness? Can't I see how we're all manifestations of love?' I look at God behind his desk, taking notes on a pad, but God's got this all wrong. We are not special. We are not crap or trash, either. We just are. We just are, and what happens just happens. And God says, 'No, that's not right.' Yeah. Well. Whatever. You can't teach God anything."

—Chuck Palahniuk

GOOD ADVICE

"A man ought to carry himself in the world as an orange tree would if it could walk up and down in the garden, swinging perfume from every little censer it holds up to the air."

—Henry Ward Beecher

SMART MOUTH: P. J. O'ROURKE

"A hat should be taken off when you greet a lady, and left off for the rest of your life. Nothing looks more stupid than a hat."

"America wasn't founded so that we could all be better. America was founded so we could all be anything we damned well pleased."

"Cleanliness becomes more important when godliness is unlikely."

"One of the annoying things about believing in free will and individual responsibility is the difficulty of finding somebody to blame your problems on. And when you do find somebody, it's remarkable how often his picture turns up on your driver's license."

"Feeling good about government is like looking on the bright side of any catastrophe. When you quit looking on the bright side, the catastrophe is still there."

"Every government is a parliament of whores. The trouble is, in a democracy, the whores are us."

ERASERHEAD

"The average pencil is seven inches long, with just a half-inch eraser—in case you thought optimism was dead."

—Robert Brault

THE RITE OF WRITING

"Many people hear voices when no one is there. Some of them are called mad and are shut up in rooms where they stare at the walls all day. Others are called writers and they do pretty much the same thing."

—Margaret Chittenden

"There is creative reading as well as creative writing."

—Ralph Waldo Emerson

"If you're going to have a complicated story, you must work to a map; otherwise you'll never make a map of it afterwards."

—J. R. R. Tolkien

"Science-fiction writers, I am sorry to say, really do not know anything. We can't talk about science, because our knowledge of it is limited and unofficial, and usually our fiction is dreadful."

—Philip K. Dick

"The faster I write, the better my output. If I'm going slow, I'm in trouble. It means I'm pushing the words instead of being pulled by them."

—Raymond Chandler

"Wanting to meet a writer because you like their books is like wanting to meet a duck because you like pâté."

—Margaret Atwood

OLD SCHOOL

"About eighty-five institutions in the Western world established by 1500 still exist in recognizable forms, with similar functions and unbroken histories, including the Catholic church, the Parliaments of the Isle of Man, of Iceland, and of Great Britain, several Swiss cantons, and seventy universities. Kings that rule, feudal lords with vassals, and guilds with monopolies are all gone. These seventy universities, however, are still in the same locations with some of the same buildings, with professors and students doing much the same things, and with governance carried on in much the same ways."

—Clark Kerr

FOREVER

"Diamonds are nothing more than chunks of coal that stuck to their jobs."

—Malcolm S. Forbes

CHAPTER 13

ARE YOU READY FOR THE COUNTRY?

"Country music has always been the best shrink that fifteen bucks can buy."

—Dierks Bentley

"You got to have smelt a lot of mule manure before you can sing like a hillbilly."

—Hank Williams

"I don't know what it's like for a book writer or a doctor or a teacher as they work to get established in their jobs. But for a singer, you've got to continue to grow or else you're just like last night's cornbread—stale and dry."

—Loretta Lynn

"After about three lessons, the voice teacher said, 'Don't take voice lessons, Johnny. Do it your way.'"

—Johnny Cash

"Ninety-nine percent of the world's lovers aren't with their first choice. That's what makes the jukebox play."

—Willie Nelson

THOUGHT FROM A PIG

"It was the best place to be, thought Wilbur, this warm delicious cellar, with the garrulous geese, the changing seasons, the heat of the sun, the passage of swallows, the nearness of rats, the sameness of sheep, the love of spiders, the smell of manure, and the glory of everything."

—E. B. White

BE CAREFUL

"There are two spiritual dangers in not owning a farm. One is the danger of supposing that breakfast comes from the grocery, and the other that heat comes from the furnace."

—Aldo Leopold

SNAPSHOTS

"Sometimes I get to places just when God's ready to have somebody click the shutter."

—Ansel Adams

"In photography there is a reality so subtle that it becomes more real than reality."

—Alfred Stieglitz

"The photographer's primary subject is light. What that light illuminates are just props."

—Jay Newman

"The moment an emotion or fact is transformed into a photograph, it is no longer a fact but an opinion. All photographs are accurate, but none of them is the truth."

—Richard Avedon

"Best wide-angle lens? Two steps backward. Look for the 'ah-ha.'"

—Ernst Haas

"I really believe there are things nobody would see if I didn't photograph them."

—Diane Arbus

IT ALL ADDS UP, PART TWO

"The laws of nature are but the mathematical thoughts of God."

—Euclid

CINEMA-SCOPE

"A film is—or should be—more like music than like fiction. It should be a progression of moods and feelings. The theme, what's behind the emotion, the meaning, all that comes later."

—Stanley Kubrick

"I'm like a navigator and I try to encourage our collaboration and find the best way that will produce fruit. I like fruit. I like cherries, I like bananas."

—Jim Jarmusch

"I think that film tends to penetrate the actor and distill the inherent quality in them that no matter what character they're playing, the film registers that quality that's sort of their essence, their soul."

—Rebecca Miller

"The way to make a film is to begin with an earthquake and work up to a climax."

—Cecil B. DeMille

"The camera is so refined that it makes it possible for us to shed light on the human soul, to reveal it more brutally and thereby add to our knowledge new dimensions of the 'real.'"

—Ingmar Bergman

"For every person who seeks fear in the real or personal sense, millions seek it vicariously, in the cinema. Give them the same pleasure they have when they wake up from a nightmare."

—Alfred Hitchcock

"My films are not the way I think things should be, but the way things are."

—Robert Altman

"If there's specific resistance to women making movies, I just choose to ignore that as an obstacle for two reasons: I can't change my gender, and I refuse to stop making movies."

—Kathryn Bigelow

TO THE POWER OF ONE

"Sometimes, when one person is missing, the whole world seems depopulated."

—**Alphonse de Lamartine**

MORE ON LIFE

"Life may have no meaning. Or even worse, it may have a meaning of which I disapprove."

—**Ashleigh Brilliant**

"When I hear somebody sigh that 'Life is hard,' I am always tempted to ask, 'Compared to what?'"

—**Sidney J. Harris**

"I came into this world black, naked, and ugly. And no matter how much I accumulate, it's a short journey. I will go out of this world black, naked, and ugly. So I enjoy life."

—**Screamin' Jay Hawkins**

"I think the life cycle is all backwards. You should die first, get it out of the way. Then you live in an old-age home. You get kicked out when you're too young, you get a gold watch, you go to work. You work forty years until you're young enough to enjoy your retirement. You do drugs, alcohol, you party, you get ready for high school. You go to grade school, you become a kid, you play, you have no responsibilities, you become a little baby, you go back into the womb, you spend your last nine months floating… and you finish off as an orgasm."

—**George Carlin**

"We have to live our lives as if we are dying of a fatal disease. Because we are."

—Phineas Narco

"Whatever you are, be a good one."

—Abraham Lincoln

SMART MOUTH: ERMA BOMBECK

"My theory on housework is, if the item doesn't multiply, smell, catch fire, or block the refrigerator door, let it be. No one else cares. Why should you?"

"One thing they never tell you about child-raising is that for the rest of your life, at the drop of a hat, you are expected to know your child's name and how old he or she is."

"It goes without saying that you should never have more children than you have car windows."

"Marriage has no guarantees. If that's what you're looking for, go live with a car battery."

"In general, my children refuse to eat anything that hasn't danced on television."

"I haven't trusted polls since I read that sixty-two percent of women had affairs during their lunch hour. I've never met a woman in my life who would give up lunch for sex."

"In two decades I've lost a total of 789 pounds. I should be hanging from a charm bracelet."

FRACTIOUS HUMANS

"A man is like a fraction whose numerator is what he is and whose denominator is what he thinks of himself. The larger the denominator, the smaller the fraction."

—Leo Tolstoy

TOLSTOY v. TYSON

"When I was in prison, I was wrapped up in all those deep books. That Tolstoy crap—people shouldn't read that stuff."

—Mike Tyson

THE CLASSICS

"Music embodies feeling without forcing it to contend and combine with thought, as it is forced in most arts and especially in the art of words."

—Franz Liszt

"The twelve notes in each octave and the variety of rhythm offer me opportunities that all of human genius will never exhaust."

—Igor Stravinsky

"I never hear in my imagination the parts successively, I hear them all at once. What a delight this is! All this inventing, this producing, takes place in a pleasing, lively dream."

—Wolfgang Amadeus Mozart

"One supreme fact which I have discovered is that it is not will-power but imagination that creates. Imagination creates reality."

—Richard Wagner

"It is not hard to compose, but what is fabulously hard is to leave the superfluous notes under the table."

—Johannes Brahms

HMMM...

"I'd rather be a lightning rod than a seismograph."

—Ken Kesey

SMART MOUTH: KURT VONNEGUT

"If you really want to disappoint your parents, and don't have the heart to be gay, go into the arts."

"Just because some of us can read and write and do a little math, that doesn't mean we deserve to conquer the universe."

"I'd rather have written one episode of *Cheers* than anything I've written."

"I want to stay as close to the edge as I can without going over. Out on the edge you see all kinds of things you can't see from the center."

"Beware of the man who works hard to learn something, learns it, and finds himself no wiser than before."

"People have to talk about something just to keep their voiceboxes in working order in case there's ever anything really meaningful to say."

"True terror is to wake up one morning and discover that your high school class is running the country."

"We're terrible animals. I think that the earth's immune system is trying to get rid of us, as well it should."

"If you can do a half-assed job of anything, you're a one-eyed man in a kingdom of the blind."

"I still believe that peace and happiness can be worked out some way. I am a fool."

ON THE BRAIN

"The seat of the soul and the control of voluntary movement—in fact, of nervous functions in general—are to be sought in the heart. The brain is an organ of minor importance."

—Aristotle

"Aristotle was famous for knowing everything. He taught that the brain exists merely to cool the blood and is not involved in the process of thinking. This is true only of certain persons."

—Will Cuppy

> Let schoolmasters puzzle their brain,
> With grammar, and nonsense, and learning,
> Good liquor, I stoutly maintain,
> Gives genius a better discerning.

—Oliver Goldsmith

"Reading, after a certain age, diverts the mind too much from its creative pursuits. Any man who reads too much and uses his own brain too little falls into lazy habits of thinking."

—Albert Einstein

"You've got the brain of a four-year-old boy, and I'll bet he was glad to get rid of it."

—Groucho Marx

"The function of the brain is to reduce all the available information and lock us into a limited experience of the world. LSD frees us from this restriction and opens us to a much larger experience."

—Stanislav Grof

"Researchers have discovered that chocolate produces some of the same reactions in the brain as marijuana. The researchers also discovered other similarities between the two but can't remember what they are."

—Matt Lauer

"Do not call for black power or green power. Call for brain power."

—Barbara Jordan

"The brain is wider than the sky."

—Emily Dickinson

"Your brain forms roughly ten thousand new cells every day, but unless they hook up to preexisting cells with strong memories, they die. Serves them right."

—Douglas Coupland

"You start chasing a ball and your brain immediately commands your body to 'Run forward, bend, scoop up the ball, peg it to the infield,' then your body says, 'Who, me?'"

—Joe DiMaggio

"If only we could pull out our brain and use only our eyes."

—Pablo Picasso

NEWS DROP

"I've tried everything. I can say to you with confidence, I know a fair amount about LSD. I've never been a social user of any of these things, but my curiosity has carried me into a lot of interesting areas."

—Dan Rather

THE BORED ROOM

"Boredom is like a pitiless zooming-in on the epidermis of time. Every instant is dilated and magnified like the pores of the face."

—Charlotte Whitton

"Boredom is a vital problem for the moralist, since at least half the sins of mankind are caused by the fear of it."

—Bertrand Russell

"It's a sad truth that everyone is a bore to someone."

—Llewellyn Miller

"I fell asleep reading a dull book and dreamed I kept on reading, so I awoke from sheer boredom."

—Heinrich Heine

"There's no excuse to be bored. Sad, yes. Angry, yes. Depressed, yes. Crazy, yes. But there's no excuse for boredom, ever."

—Viggo Mortensen

"Boredom is just the reverse side of fascination: both depend on being outside rather than inside a situation, and one leads to the other."

—Susan Sontag

"I begin with the principle that all men are bores. Surely no one will prove himself so great a bore as to contradict me in this."

—Søren Kierkegaard

MOVERS AND SHAKERS

We are the music-makers,
And we are the dreamers of dreams,
Wandering by lone sea-breakers,
And sitting by desolate streams;
World-losers and world-forsakers,
On whom the pale moon gleams:
Yet we are the movers and shakers
Of the world for ever, it seems.

—Arthur William Edgar O'Shaughnessy

ON INSECTS

"If all mankind were to disappear, the world would regenerate back to the rich state of equilibrium that existed ten thousand years ago. If insects were to vanish, the environment would collapse into chaos."

—Edward O. Wilson

"Human knowledge will be erased from the world's archives before we possess the last word that a gnat has to say to us."

—Jean-Henri Fabre

"Teaching a child not to step on a caterpillar is as valuable to the child as it is to the caterpillar."

—Bradley Miller

"I always felt that insects are the general rule, and everything else is a special case."

—Paul Bystrak

"We hope that, when the insects take over the world, they will remember with gratitude how we took them along on all our picnics."

—Richard Vaughan

SMART MOUTH: DAVID LETTERMAN

"Thanksgiving is the day when...my mom, after six Bloody Marys, looks at the turkey and goes: 'Here kitty, kitty.'"

"Charlton Heston admitted he had a drinking problem, and I said to myself, 'Thank God this guy doesn't own any guns!'"

"You can tell it's the Christmas season. Stores are selling off their expired milk as eggnog."

"You can e-mail me, but I prefer letters that come through conventional mail. I like letters that have been licked by strangers."

"7-Eleven now has edible straws to go with their Slurpees. If they want something edible, why not start with the hot dogs?"

"I was in the polling place today, and honest to God, I see a guy stick his head out of the curtains. And he's holding a pair of pants and he says, 'Can I get these in a forty-six?'"

"New York now leads the world's great cities in the number of people around whom you shouldn't make a sudden move."

"Congratulations are in order for Woody Allen —he and Soon Yi have a brand-new baby daughter. It's all part of Woody's plan to grow his own wives."

AH ONE, AH TWO...

"Of all noises, I think music is the least disagreeable."

—Samuel Johnson

"To hell with reality! I want to die in music, not in reason or in prose. People don't deserve the restraint we show by not going into delirium in front of them. To hell with them!"

—Louis-Ferdinand Celine

"Songs are funny things. They can slip across borders. Proliferate in prisons. Penetrate hard shells. I always believed that the right song at the right moment could change history."

—Pete Seeger

"A painter paints his picture on canvas. But musicians paint their pictures on silence. We provide the music. You provide the silence."

—Leopold Stokowski

"Hell is full of musical amateurs."

—George Bernard Shaw

"Music is a means of rapid transportation."

—John Cage

"If I were not a physicist, I would probably be a musician. I often think in music. I live my daydreams in music. I see my life in terms of music."

—Albert Einstein

AND NOW A WORD
FROM OUR SPONSORS

"Advertising is a valuable economic factor because it is the cheapest way of selling goods, particularly if the goods are worthless."

—Sinclair Lewis

"You can tell the ideals of a nation by its advertisements."

—Norman Douglas

"Advertising is the modern substitute for argument; its function is to make the worse appear the better."

—George Santayana

"It is a most extraordinary thing, but I never read a patent medicine advertisement without being impelled to the conclusion that I am suffering from the particular disease therein dealt with in its most virulent form."

—Jerome K. Jerome

"I have always believed that writing advertisements is the second most profitable form of writing. The first, of course, is ransom notes."

—Philip Dusenberry

"Advertising is the greatest art form of the twentieth century."

—Marshall McLuhan

"If advertisers spent the same amount of money on improving their products as they do on advertising, then they wouldn't have to advertise them."

—Will Rogers

"Our society's values are being corrupted by advertising's insistence on the equation: Youth equals popularity, popularity equals success, success equals happiness."

—John Arbuthnot Fisher

"So long as there's a jingle in your head, television isn't free."

—Jason Love

"Man is at his vilest when he erects a billboard. When I retire from Madison Avenue, I am going to start a secret society of masked vigilantes who will travel around the world on silent motor bicycles, chopping down posters at the dark of the moon. How many juries will convict us when we are caught in these acts of beneficent citizenship?"

—David Ogilvy

GOOD TO REMEMBER

"A defining attribute of witch-hunting is the way the momentum builds. It's very hard to stop beyond a certain point—because beyond a certain point, if you say 'Stop!' they'll call you a witch."

—John Putnam Demos

CHAPTER 14

WILBUR WRONG

"I confess that in 1901, I said to my brother Orville that man would not fly for fifty years. Ever since, I have distrusted myself and avoided all predictions."

—Wilbur Wright

ON GRAMMAR AND PUNCTUATION

"The older I grow, the less important the comma becomes. Let the reader catch his own breath."

—Elizabeth Clarkson Zwart

"An excessive use of exclamation marks is a certain indication of an unpracticed writer or of one who wants to add a spurious dash of sensation to something unsensational."

—H. W. Fowler

"Let me be plain: the semicolon is ugly, ugly as a tick on a dog's belly. I pinch them out of my prose."

—Donald Barthelme

"It would be nice if one day the number of apostrophes properly placed in it's equaled exactly the number of apostrophes properly omitted from its, instead of the other way round."

—Lynne Truss

"Grammar is a piano I play by ear. All I know about grammar is its power."

—Joan Didion

"When I split an infinitive, god damn it, I split it so it stays split."

—Raymond Chandler

IT DOESN'T MATTER

"One day Alice came to a fork in the road and saw a Cheshire cat in a tree. 'Which road do I take?' she asked. 'Where do you want to go?' was his response. 'I don't know,' Alice answered. 'Then,' said the cat, 'it doesn't matter.'"

—Lewis Carroll, *Alice's Adventures in Wonderland*

CHEESE SPOKEN HERE

"Nothing says 'holidays' like a cheese log."

—Ellen DeGeneres

"Swiss cheese is a rip-off. It's the only cheese you can bite into and miss."

—Mitch Hedberg

"What happens to the hole when the cheese is gone?"

—**Bertolt Brecht**

"When cheese gets its picture taken, what does it say?"

—**George Carlin**

"I went into a French restaurant and asked the waiter, 'Have you got frog's legs?' He said, 'Yes,' so I said, 'Well, hop into the kitchen and get me a cheese sandwich.'"

—**Tommy Cooper**

"Cheese—milk's leap toward immortality."

—**Clifton Fadiman**

DON'T WORRY...

"Worry is today's mice nibbling on tomorrow's cheese."

—**Anonymous**

"Worry is rust upon the blade."

—**Henry Ward Hughes**

"Some men storm imaginary Alps all their lives, and die in the foothills cursing difficulties which do not exist."

—**Edgar Watson Howe**

Some of your hurts you have cured,
And the sharpest you still have survived,
But what torments of grief you endured
From the evil which never arrived.

—**Ralph Waldo Emerson**

MORE WRITERS ON WRITING

"A story must have a beginning, a middle, and an end, but not necessarily in that order."

—Jean-Luc Godard

"An author in his book must be like God in the universe: present everywhere and visible nowhere."

—Gustave Flaubert

"Anybody who likes writing a book is an idiot. Because it's impossible—it's like having a homework assignment every stinking day until it's done. And when it's done and you're sitting there reading it, you realize the 12,000 things you didn't do. And when people read it, they tell you, 'Well, gee, I'm not interested.' 'Great, I'm glad I wrote this!'"

—Lewis Black

TOIL AND TROUBLE

"It's a shame that a man can't eat for eight hours; he can't drink for eight hours; he can't make love for eight hours. The only thing a man can do for eight hours is work."

—William Faulkner

"Work is accomplished by those employees who have not yet reached their level of incompetence."

—Laurence J. Peter

"Nighttime is really the best time to work. All the ideas are there to be yours because everyone else is asleep."

—Catherine O'Hara

"If hard work were such a wonderful thing, surely the rich would have kept it all to themselves."

—Lane Kirkland

"Oh, you hate your job? Why didn't you say so? There's a support group for that. It's called *everybody*, and they meet at the bar."

—Drew Carey

SMART MOUTH: C. S. LEWIS

"Experience: that most brutal of teachers. But you learn, my God do you learn."

"Courage is not simply one of the virtues, but the form of every virtue at the testing point."

"Affection is responsible for nine-tenths of whatever solid and durable happiness there is in our lives."

"Nothing that you have not given away will ever be really yours."

"With the possible exception of the equator, everything begins somewhere."

"It may be hard for an egg to turn into a bird: It would be a sight harder for it to learn to fly while remaining an egg. We are like eggs at present. And you cannot go on indefinitely being just an ordinary, decent egg. We must be hatched or go bad."

"Friendship is born at that moment when one person says to another: 'What! You too? I thought I was the only one.'"

WITH INTEREST

"Once I was in Victoria, and I saw a very large house. They told me it was a bank and that the white men place their money there to be taken care of, and that by and by they got it back with interest. We are Indians and we have no such bank; but when we have plenty of money or blankets, we give them away to other chiefs and people, and by and by they return them with interest, and our hearts feel good. Our way of giving is our bank."

—Chief Maquinna, Nuu-chah-nulth tribe, British Columbia

QUOTES TO READ TOMORROW

"Don't fool yourself that important things can be put off till tomorrow; they can be put off forever, or not at all."

—Mignon McLaughlin

"One of the greatest labor-saving inventions of today is tomorrow."

—Vincent T. Foss

"How does a project get to be a year behind schedule? One day at a time."

—Fred Brooks

"My mother always told me I wouldn't amount to anything because I procrastinate. I said, 'Just wait!'"

—Judy Tenuta

"One thing that's good about procrastination is that you always have something planned for tomorrow."

—G. B. Stern

I HATE THAT

"The strangest and most fantastic fact about negative emotions
is that people actually worship them."

—P. D. Ouspensky

MY NAME IS MR.

"I thought about my father being called 'boy,' my uncle being
called 'boy,' my brother being called 'boy.' What does a black
man have to do before he's given respect as a man?' So when
I was eighteen years old, I said I was old enough to be called a
man. I self-ordained myself 'Mr. T' so the first word out of everybody's mouth is 'Mister.' That's a sign of respect that my father
didn't get."

—Mr. T

COLLEGE CREDITS

"College: A place where pebbles are polished and diamonds are
dimmed."

—Robert G. Ingersoll

"College is a place to keep warm between high school and an
early marriage."

—George Gobel

"College is a refuge from hasty judgment."

—Robert Frost

"Fathers send their sons to college either because they went to
college or they didn't."

—L. L. Hendren

"Of course there's a lot of knowledge in universities: the freshmen bring a little in; the seniors don't take much away, so knowledge sort of accumulates."

—Abbott Lawrence Lowell

IF LIFE GIVES YOU LEMONS...

"If life gives you a bowl of lemons, go find an annoying guy with paper cuts."

—Anonymous

"If life gives you lemons, make grape juice. Then sit back and let the world wonder how you did it."

—Anonymous

"WOOF!" PART TWO

"People teach their dogs to sit; it's a trick. I've been sitting my whole life, and a dog has never looked at me as though he thought I was tricky."

—Mitch Hedberg

"Loving a dog is one thing, humanizing and pampering the animal is another. It's a selfish attitude because it's what the human wants, instead of really seeing the picture—what does the dog need?"

—Cesar Millan

"From the dog's point of view, his master is an elongated and abnormally cunning dog."

—Mabel Louise Robinson

"A dog has the soul of a philosopher."

—Plato

"Ever consider what they must think of us? I mean, here we come back from a grocery store with the most amazing haul—chicken, pork, half a cow. They must think we're the greatest hunters on earth!"

—Anne Tyler

"Dogs' lives are too short. Their only fault, really."

—Agnes Sligh Turnbull

CHEFS ON COOKING

"The problem with cooking is too many rules. You don't have to have perfect squares. Who cares, you know? Like we got some architect judging us at breakfast!"

—Emeril Lagasse

"The discovery of a new dish does more for the happiness of mankind than the discovery of a star."

—Jean Brillat-Savarin

"From an early age I understood that cooking was never going to be a job, it's a passion."

—Gordon Ramsay

"Only cook and eat food with people you like. Life's too short for bad food and bad company."

—Rocco DiSpirito

IS IT SAFE?

"A ship is safe in harbor, but that is not what ships are for."

—William Shedd

INSULTS: ON FILM

"It isn't that I don't like you, Susan, because after all, in moments of quiet, I'm strangely drawn toward you. But, well, there haven't been any quiet moments."

—Dr. Huxley (Cary Grant), *Bringing Up Baby*

"There's a name for you ladies, but it isn't used in high society, outside of a kennel."

—Crystal Allen (Joan Crawford), *The Women*

"Well, that covers a lot of ground. Say! You cover a lot of ground yourself. You'd better beat it. I hear they're gonna tear you down and put up an office building where you're standing. You know, you haven't stopped talking since I came here. You must have been vaccinated with a phonograph needle."

—Groucho Marx, *Duck Soup*

"You cheap, lying, no good, rotten, floor-flushing, low-life, snake-licking, dirt-eating, inbred, overstuffed, ignorant, blood-sucking, dog-kissing, brainless, di**less, hopeless, heartless, fatass, bug-eyed, stiff-legged, spineless, worm-headed sack of monkey sh*t!"

—Clark Griswold (Chevy Chase),
National Lampoon's Christmas Vacation

"I seen your mother kicking a can down the street. I said 'What you doin'?' and she said 'Moving.'"

—Sidney Deane (Wesley Snipes),
White Men Can't Jump

"Benjamin is nobody's friend. If Benjamin were an ice cream flavor, he'd be pralines and di**."

—Garth Algar (Dana Carvey), *Wayne's World*

HMMM...

"Now those guys can sit naked in the snow at 18,000 feet and they have such powers of mental discipline that if they put their mind to it, hell, they can generate enough heat to melt snow for twenty feet around. Now you put that Tibetan priest on the mound, naked or not, with a baseball in his palm, and he'll take that power of concentration and make the ball disappear and then materialize down the line in the catcher's mitt. There's my idea of a relief pitcher."

—Bill Lee (Boston Red Sox)

L'CHAIM!

"You can't drink all day if you don't start in the morning."

—On the label of Founder's Breakfast Stout

"Do not allow children to mix drinks. It is unseemly...and they use too much vermouth."

—Steve Allen

"A meal of bread, cheese, and beer constitutes the perfect food."

—Queen Elizabeth I

Filled with mingled cream and amber;
I will drain that glass again.
Most peculiar visions clamber
through the chamber of my brain.
Quaintest thoughts, queerest fancies,
come to life, and fade away.
What care I how time advances?
I am drinking ale today.

—Edgar Allan Poe

"If you ever reach total enlightenment while drinking beer, I bet it makes beer shoot out your nose."

—Jack Handey

"Give me a woman who truly loves beer and I will conquer the world."

—Kaiser Wilhelm II

"People who drink light 'beer' don't like the taste of beer; they just like to pee a lot."

—Anonymous

"Nothing ever tasted better than a cold beer on a beautiful afternoon with nothing to look forward to than more of the same."

—Hugh Hood

THIRST FOR IGNORANCE

"Thirst for existence, O monks, has a specific condition, it is nourished by something, it also does not go without support. And what is that nourishment? It is ignorance."

—Buddha

SMART MOUTH: NORM FROM *CHEERS*!

Woody: "Can I draw you a beer, Norm?"
Norm: "No, I know what they look like. Just pour me one."

Coach: What'll it be, Normie?"
Norm: "Just the usual, Coach. I'll have a froth of beer and a snorkel."

Sam: "What'll you have, Normie?"
Norm: "Well, I'm in a gambling mood, Sammy. I'll take a glass of whatever comes out of that tap."
Sam: "Looks like beer, Norm."
Norm: "Call me Mister Lucky."

Woody: "What's the story, Mr. Peterson?"
Norm: "The Bobbsey twins go to the brewery. Let's cut to the happy ending."

Woody: "Can I pour you a beer, Mr. Peterson?"

Norm: "A little early isn't it, Woody?"
Woody: "For a beer?"
Norm: "No, for stupid questions."
Sam: "How's about a beer, Norm?"
Norm: "That's that amber sudsy stuff, right? I've heard good things about it!"

HAVE A NICE DAY

"The earth has a skin and that skin has diseases; one of its diseases is called Man."

—Friedrich Nietzsche

"To perceive is to suffer."

—Aristotle

"Nature is that lovely lady to whom we owe polio, leprosy, smallpox, syphilis, tuberculosis, and cancer."

—Stanley N. Cohen

"Inside every cynical person there is a disappointed idealist."

—George Carlin

"Until we stop harming all other living beings, we are still savages."

—Thomas Edison

"The earth swarms with people who are not worth talking to."

—Voltaire

"Human beings will line up for miles to buy a bucket of catastrophes, but don't try selling sunshine and light; you'll go broke."

—Chuck Jones

MIRRORS

"When you use bronze as a mirror, you can straighten your clothes and hat. When you use antiquity as a mirror, you can see the waxing and waning. When you use a person as a mirror, you can know if you grasp things or not. Wei Zheng is gone; I have lost my mirror."

—Chinese emperor Taizong (599-649), on his minister Wei Zheng

SMART MOUTH: MARGARET ATWOOD

"I became a poet at the age of sixteen. I did not intend to do it. It was not my fault."

"I've never understood why people consider youth a time of freedom and joy. It's probably because they have forgotten their own."

"Another belief of mine: that everyone else my age is an adult, whereas I am merely in disguise."

"The answers you get from literature depend on the questions you pose."

"It's a feature of our age that if you write a work of fiction, everyone assumes that the people and events in it are disguised biography—but if you write your biography, it's equally assumed you're lying your head off."

> She has been condemned to death by hanging. A man may escape this death by becoming the hangman, a woman by marrying the hangman. But at the present time there is no hangman; thus there is no escape. There is only a death, indefinitely postponed. This is not fantasy, it is history.

CHAPTER 15

IF THE CROWN FITS

"I always try to dance when this song comes on because I am the queen and I like to dance."

**—Queen Elizabeth II, to startled onlookers
when she started dancing to ABBA's
"Dancing Queen" at a dinner party**

REVENGE

"Revenge is always the weak pleasure of a little and narrow mind."

—Juvenal

"Revenge is sweet and not fattening."

—Alfred Hitchcock

"Revenge is an act of passion; vengeance of justice. Injuries are revenged; crimes are avenged."

—Samuel Johnson

"Revenge is profitable, gratitude is expensive."

—Edward Gibbon

"If an injury has to be done to a man, it should be so severe that his vengeance need not be feared."

—Niccolo Machiavelli

"Evil is always devising more corrosive misery through man's restless need to exact revenge out of his hate."

—Ralph Steadman

"I felt so painfully isolated that I vowed I would get revenge on the world by becoming a famous cartoonist."

—R. Crumb

"May we not succumb to thoughts of violence and revenge today, but rather to thoughts of mercy and compassion. We are to love our enemies that they might be returned to their right minds."

—Marianne Williamson

"Something of vengeance I had tasted for the first time; as aromatic wine it seemed, on swallowing, warm and racy: its after-flavor, metallic and corroding, gave me a sensation as if I had been poisoned."

—Charlotte Brontë

"There is no revenge so complete as forgiveness."

—Josh Billings

LOVE'S OLD SWEET SONG

Just a song at twilight,
When the lights are low;
And the flick'ring shadows,
Softly come and go,
Tho' the heart be weary,
Sad the day and long,
Still to us at twilight,
Comes love's old song,
Comes love's old sweet song.

—Clifton Bingham

LOOK...

"Look deep into nature, and then you will understand everything better."

—Albert Einstein

"Look at life through the windshield, not the rearview mirror"

—Byrd Baggett

"But the eyes are blind. One must look with the heart."

—Antoine de Saint-Exupéry

"Take a look at your natural river. What are you? Stop playing games with yourself. Where's your river going? Are you riding with it? Or are you rowing against it? Don't you see that there is no effort if you're riding with your river?"

—Frederick (Carl) Frieseke

Look thy last on all things lovely,
Every hour—let no night
Seal thy sense in deathly slumber
Till to delight
Thou hast paid thy utmost blessing.

—Walter de la Mare

"The girl gave him a look which ought to have stuck at least four inches out of his back."

—Raymond Chandler

OBSESSION

"That's the thing about girls. Every time they do something pretty, even if they're not much to look at, or even if they're sort of stupid, you fall in love with them, and then you never know where the hell you are. Girls. Jesus Christ. They can drive you crazy. They really can."

—J. D. Salinger, *The Catcher in the Rye*

ON ATHEISM

"All children are atheists. They have no idea of God."

—Paul-Henri, Baron d'Holbach

"The philosophy of Atheism represents a concept of life without any metaphysical Beyond or Divine Regulator. It is the concept of an actual, real world with its liberating, expanding and beautifying possibilities, as against an unreal world, which, with its spirits, oracles, and mean contentment has kept humanity in helpless degradation."

—Emma Goldman

"Atheism is a way of humility. It's to think oneself to be an animal, as we are actually and to allow oneself to become human."

—André Comte-Sponville

"I once wanted to become an atheist, but I gave up—they have no holidays."

—Henny Youngman

"If there were no God, there would be no atheists."

—G. K. Chesterton

LOST IN THE MAIL

"It is said that as many days as there are in the whole journey, so many are the men and horses that stand along the road, each horse and man at the interval of a day's journey; and these are stayed neither by snow nor rain nor heat nor darkness from accomplishing their appointed course with all speed."

—Herodotus (5th century BCE)

GRASS

"Every blade of grass has its angel that bends over it and whispers, 'Grow, grow.'"

—the Talmud

"Knowing trees, I understand the meaning of patience. Knowing grass, I can appreciate persistence."

—Hal Borland

"The moment one gives close attention to any thing, even a blade of grass, it becomes a mysterious, awesome, indescribably magnificent world in itself."

—Henry Miller

"And God said, Let the earth bring forth grass, and the earth brought forth grass, and the Rastafarians smoked it."

—Spike Milligan

A REMINDER

"Every happy man should have someone with a little hammer at his door to knock and remind him that there are unhappy people, and that, however happy he may be, life will sooner or later show its claws."

—Anton Chekhov

THIRTEEN NOVEL NOVEL OPENINGS

"Into the face of the young man who sat on the terrace of the Hotel Magnifique at Cannes there had crept a look of furtive shame, the shifty, hangdog look which announces that an Englishman is about to talk French."

—*The Luck of the Bodkins*, P. G. Wodehouse

"Many years later, as he faced the firing squad, Colonel Aureliano Buendía was to remember that distant afternoon when his father took him to discover ice."

—*One Hundred Years of Solitude*, Gabriel García Márquez

"Lolita, light of my life, fire of my loins."

—*Lolita*, Vladimir Nabokov

"Was anyone hurt?"

—*A Handful of Dust*, Evelyn Waugh

"On my naming day when I come 12 I gone front spear and kilt a wyld boar he parbly ben the las wyld pig on the Bundel Downs any how there hadnt ben none for a long time befor him nor I aint looking to see none agen."

—*Riddley Walker*, Russell Hoban

"Once upon a time and a very good time it was there was a moocow coming down along the road and this moocow that was coming down along the road met a nicens little boy named baby tuckoo."

—*A Portrait of the Artist as a Young Man*, James Joyce

"All this happened, more or less."

—*Slaughterhouse-Five*, Kurt Vonnegut

"A green hunting cap squeezed the top of the fleshy balloon of a head."

—*A Confederacy of Dunces*, John Kennedy Toole

"The drought had lasted now for ten million years, and the reign of the terrible lizards had long since ended. Here on the Equator, in the continent which would one day be known as Africa, the battle for existence had reached a new climax of ferocity, and the victor was not yet in sight."

—*2001: A Space Odyssey*, Arthur C. Clarke

"It was love at first sight. The first time Yossarian saw the chaplain he fell madly in love with him."

—*Catch-22*, Joseph Heller

"My father's family name being Pirrip, and my Christian name Philip, my infant tongue could make of both names nothing longer or more explicit than Pip. So, I called myself Pip, and came to be called Pip."

—*Great Expectations*, Charles Dickens

"On they went, singing 'Eternal Memory,' and whenever they stopped, the sound of their feet, the horses and the gusts of wind seemed to carry on their singing."

—*Doctor Zhivago*, Boris Pasternak

"Mother died today. Or maybe yesterday, I don't know."

—*The Stranger*, Albert Camus

I PLEDGE ALLEGIANCE

"What is patriotism but the love of the food one ate as a child?"

—Lin Yutang

"What do we mean by patriotism in the context of our times? I venture to suggest that what we mean is a sense of national responsibility...a patriotism which is not short, frenzied outbursts of emotion, but the tranquil and steady dedication of a lifetime."

—Adlai Stevenson

"No matter that patriotism is too often the refuge of scoundrels. Dissent, rebellion, and all-around hell-raising remain the true duty of patriots."

—Barbara Ehrenreich

"'My country, right or wrong' is a thing no patriot would ever think of saying except in a desperate case. It is like saying 'My mother, drunk or sober.'"

—G. K. Chesterton

"The love of one's country is a splendid thing. But why should love stop at the border?"

—Pablo Casals

THE BEGINNING OF WISDOM

"The beginning of wisdom is to call things by their right names."

—Chinese proverb

LOTTERY BLUES

"Common sense is just as good a critic of the lottery as any statistical breakdown."

—Hunter Baker

"All are inclined to believe what they covet, from a lottery-ticket up to a passport to Paradise."

—Lord Byron

"I've done the calculation and your chances of winning the lottery are identical whether you play or not."

—Fran Lebowitz

"A lottery is properly a tax upon unfortunate, self-conceited fools. The Sovereign should have guard of these fools, even as in the case of lunatics and idiots."

—Sir William Petty

"There are multitudes whose life is nothing but a continuous lottery; who are always within a few months of plenty and happiness, and how often soever they are mocked with blanks, expect a prize from the next adventure."

—Samuel Johnson

"If you really want something in life you have to work for it. Now quiet, they're about to announce the lottery numbers."

—Homer Simpson

NOTHING

Heaven does nothing: its non-doing is its serenity.
Earth does nothing: its non-doing is its rest.
From the union of these two non-doings
All actions proceed,
All things are made.
How vast, how invisible
This coming-to-be!
All things come from nowhere!
How vast, how invisible—
No way to explain it!
All beings in their perfection
Are born of non-doing.
Hence it is said:
"Heaven and earth do nothing
Yet there is nothing they do not do."
Where is the man who can attain
To this non-doing?

—Thomas Merton, *The Way of Chuang Tzu*

SHHH...

"The word you keep between your lips is your slave. The word you speak is your master."

—Arabic proverb

EMERGENCY ROOM

"Hospitals are places that you have to stay in for a long time, even if you are a visitor. Time doesn't seem to pass in the same way in hospitals as it does in other places. Time seems to almost not exist in the same way as it does in other places."

—Pedro Almodovar

"A trip to the hospital is always a descent into the macabre. I have never trusted a place with shiny floors."

—Terry Tempest Williams

"Looking out a hospital window is different from looking out of any other. Somehow, you do not see outside."

—Carol Matthau

"A hospital is a parked taxi with the meter running."

—Groucho Marx

"In hospitals, there is no time off for good behavior."

—Josephine Tey

"Getting out of the hospital is a lot like resigning from a book club. You're not out of it until the computer says you're out of it."

—Erma Bombeck

COLORS

"Of all the hues, reds have the most potency. If there is one electric blue, a dozen reds are so charged. Use them to punctuate white, burn into bronzes, or dynamite black."

—Jack Lenor Larsen

"Orange is the happiest color."

—Frank Sinatra

"What a horrible thing yellow is."

—Edgar Degas

"Absolute green is the most restful color, lacking any undertone of joy, grief, or passion. On exhausted men this restfulness has a beneficial effect, but after a time it becomes tedious."

—Wassily Kandinsky

"Violet has the shortest wavelength of the spectrum. Behind it, the invisible ultraviolet. Roses are red, violets are blue. Poor violet, violated for a rhyme."

—Derek Jarman

"Today, O lovely woman in dress dyed indigo,
O dress, your thread is indigo saturated today."

—From a Hadrami (Yemeni) wedding song

"Mauve? Mauve is just pink trying to be purple."

—James Abbot McNeill Whistler

"Blue is the only color which maintains its own character in all its tones…it will always stay blue; whereas yellow is blackened in its shades, and fades away when lightened; red when darkened becomes brown, and diluted with white is no longer red but another color—pink."

—Raoul Dufy

"If time were a color, I bet it would be a tasteful off-white."

—Greg Parrish

UNDERSTANDING

"To understand what another person is saying, you must assume that it is true and try to imagine what it could be true of."

—George A. Miller

REMEMBER THIS

"A memory is what is left when something happens and does not completely unhappen."

—Edward de Bono

One need not be a chamber to be haunted;
One need not be a house;
The brain has corridors surpassing
Material place.

—Emily Dickinson

"Every man's memory is his private literature."

—Aldous Huxley

"Life is a rough biography. Memories smooth out the edges."

—Dante G. Roque

"The faintest waft is sometimes enough to induce feelings of hunger or anticipation, or to transport you back through time and space to a long-forgotten moment in your childhood. It can overwhelm you in an instant or simply tease you, creeping into your consciousness slowly and evaporating almost the moment it is detected."

—Stephen Lacey

"Everybody needs his memories. They keep the wolf of insignificance from the door."

—Saul Bellow

FOLDS

What Do I Know About Zen?
Better to think
less, or more
truly, perhaps, more
like a fold in a piece
of white paper,
line or end
or edge, dividing two
that look the same.

—Amy Miller

CHAPTER 16

HEROES AT HOME

"The grandest of heroic deeds are those which are performed within four walls and in domestic property."

—Jean Paul Richter

SMART MOUTH: STEPHEN FRY

"An original idea can't be too hard. The library must be full of them."

"Secret vices? I don't know. Rather too fond of chocolate. My wife tells me I overdo the heroin. Otherwise, not really."

"It is a cliché that most clichés are true, but then like most clichés, that cliché is untrue."

"I don't need you to remind me of my age. I have a bladder to do that for me."

"If ignorance is bliss, why aren't there more happy people in the world?"

"If I had a large amount of money I should found a hospital for those whose grip upon the world is so tenuous that they can be severely offended by words and phrases yet remain all unoffended by the injustice, violence, and oppression that howls daily."

"You should try the fruit of every tree of every garden in the world. But 'try' is the word. Some fruits will be rotten, some will be poisonous, and some will be so seductive you eat nothing else and become malnutreated, if there is such a word."

"Smell is the most deeply embarrassing of all the five senses, the one which most clearly tells us precisely who and what we are."

FROM THE GYM

"If God invented marathons to keep people from doing anything more stupid, Ironman triathlons must have taken him completely by surprise."

—**P. Z. Pearce**

"Melancholy is incompatible with bicycling."

—**James E. Starrs**

"I consider exercise vulgar. It makes people smell."

—**Alec Yuill-Thornton**

"People say that losing weight is no walk in the park. When I hear that, I think, 'Yeah, that's the problem.'"

—**Chris Adams**

FROM THE GARDEN

Roses are red,
Violets are blue;
But they don't get around
Like the dandelions do.

—**Slim Acres**

WHY OH WHY?

"Why is the alphabet in that order? Is it because of that song?"

—**Steven Wright**

"Why is the word 'abbreviation' so long?"

—**Jerry Seinfeld**

"Why is there so much month left at the end of the money?"

—**John Barrymore**

"If truth is beauty, how come no one has their hair done in the library?"

—**Lily Tomlin**

"If you can't live without me, why aren't you dead already?"

—**Cynthia Heimel**

"Well, if I called the wrong number, why did you answer the phone?"

—James Thurber

"He who has a why can endure any how."

—Friedrich Nietzsche

"I wept when I was born…and every day explains why."

—Spanish proverb

GRAND SLAM

"The team playing behind Sandy Koufax is the ghastliest scoring team in history. They pile up runs at the rate of one every nine innings. This is a little like making Rembrandt paint on the back of cigar boxes, giving Paderewski a piano with two octaves, Caruso singing with a high school chorus. With the Babe Ruth Yankees, Sandy Koufax would have been the first undefeated pitcher in history."

—Jim Murray

MORE FROM THE BOYS AND GIRLS

"Here's all you have to know about men and women: women are crazy, men are stupid. And the main reason women are crazy is that men are stupid."

—George Carlin

"Why are women so much more interesting to men then men are to women?"

—Virginia Woolf

"The only thing worse than a man you can't control is a man you can."

—Jean Kerr

"If men can run the world, why can't they stop wearing neckties? How intelligent is it to start the day by tying a little noose around your neck?"

—Linda Ellerbee

"Male and female represent the two sides of the great radical dualism. But in fact they are perpetually passing into one another. Fluid hardens to solid, solid rushes to fluid. There is no wholly masculine man, no purely feminine woman."

—Margaret Fuller

"A pessimist is a man who thinks all women are bad. An optimist is a man who hopes they are."

—Chauncey Mitchell Depew

GOOD ADVICE

"If you know how to cheat, start now."

—Earl Weaver

"The best way to win an argument is to begin by being right."

—Jill Ruckelshaus

"If you're going to do something tonight that you'll be sorry for tomorrow, sleep late."

—Henny Youngman

"Appear weak when you are strong, and strong when you are weak."

—**Sun Tzu**

"If it has tires or testicles, you're going to have trouble with it."

—**Linda Furney**

"Be happy. It's one way of being wise."

—**Sidonie-Gabrielle Colette**

"My advice to you is not to inquire why or whither but just enjoy your ice cream while it's on your plate."

—**Thornton Wilder**

"In dwelling, live close to the ground. In thinking, keep to the simple. In conflict, be fair and generous. In governing, don't try to control. In work, do what you enjoy. In family life, be completely present."

—**Lao Tzu**

"Laugh at yourself first, before anyone else can."

—**Elsa Maxwell**

THE POWER OF GLASSES

"If the eye does not want to see, neither light nor glasses will help."

—**German proverb**

"The greatest magnifying glasses in the world are a man's own eyes when they look upon his own person."

—**Alexander Pope**

"With my sunglasses on, I'm Jack Nicholson. Without them, I'm fat and sixty."

—Jack Nicholson

WISDOM, BEAUTY, AND BALANCE

"Besides the noble art of getting things done, there is the noble art of leaving things undone. The wisdom of life consists in the elimination of nonessentials."

—Lin Yutang

"Everything has beauty, though not everyone sees it."

—Confucius

"Whether you go up the ladder or down it, your position is shaky. When you stand with your two feet on the ground, you will always keep your balance."

—*Tao Te Ching*

YOU'VE GOT A FRIEND

"Friendship is a sheltering tree."

—Samuel Taylor Coleridge

"Friendship multiplies the good of life and divides the evil."

—Baltasar Gracián

"Friendship marks a life even more deeply than love. Love risks degenerating into obsession; friendship is never anything but sharing."

—Elie Wiesel

"Am I not destroying my enemies when I make friends of them?"

—Abraham Lincoln

"It is one of the blessings of old friends that you can afford to be stupid with them."

—Ralph Waldo Emerson

"When all is said and done, friendship is the only trustworthy fabric of the affections. Love is a delirious inhuman state of mind: when hot it substitutes indulgence for fair play; when cold it is cruel, but friendship is warmth in cold, firm ground in a bog."

—Miles Franklin

MORE OLD-TIME COMEDY

"I don't like country music, but I don't mean to denigrate those who do. And for the people who like country music, denigrate means 'put down.'"

—Bob Newhart

"A fellow told me he was going to hang-glider school. He said, 'I've been going for three months.' I said, 'How many successful jumps do you need to make before you graduate?' He said, 'All of them.'"

—Red Skelton

"I have enough money to last me the rest of my life, unless I buy something."

—Jackie Mason

"A guy bought a farm. He didn't know anything about farms, but he bought one anyway. He decides he's going to plant something. Anything. 'What are you going to plant?' his friend asks. 'Razor blades and cabbages.' His friend looks at him. 'Razor blades and cabbages? What could you possibly get out of that?' 'Coleslaw.'"

—Buddy Hackett

WE, ROBOT

"In the next century it will be the early mechanical bird which gets the first plastic worm out of the artificial grass."

—William E. Vaughan

ON THE ROLE OF GOVERNMENT

"The role of the government ought to be like the role of a referee in boxing, keeping the big guys from killing the little guys. But today the government has cast down its duty, and media competition is less like boxing and more like professional wrestling: The wrestler and the referee are both kicking the guy on the canvas."

—Ted Turner

GAY PRIDE

"Homosexuality is God's way of ensuring that the truly gifted aren't burdened with children."

—Sam Austin

"The Bible contains six admonishments to homosexuals and 362 admonishments to heterosexuals. That doesn't mean that God doesn't love heterosexuals. It's just that they need more supervision."

—Lynn Lavner

"My lesbianism is an act of Christian charity. All those women out there praying for a man, and I'm giving them my share."

—**Rita Mae Brown**

AND HE MEANS IT

"When you give a lesson in meanness to a critter or a person, don't be surprised if they learn their lesson."

—**Will Rogers**

THE PRESIDENTS' LAST WORDS

"I die hard, but am not afraid to go."

—**George Washington (1799)**

"Is it the Fourth?"

—**Thomas Jefferson (July 4, 1826)**

"I always talk better lying down."

—**James Madison (1836)**

"Oh, do not cry. Be good children and we will all meet in heaven."

—**Andrew Jackson (1845)**

"This is the last of earth. I am content."

—**John Quincy Adams (1848)**

"I love you, Sarah. For all eternity, I love you."

—**James K. Polk, to his wife (1849)**

Mary Todd Lincoln: "What will Miss Harris think of my hanging on to you so?"
Abraham Lincoln: "She won't think anything about it."

**—While watching the play
at the Ford Theater (1865)**

"History will vindicate my memory."

—James Buchanan (1868)

"The nourishment is palatable."

—Millard Fillmore (1874)

"Water."

—Ulysses S. Grant (1885)

"Put out the light."

—Theodore Roosevelt (1919)

"I am ready."

—Woodrow Wilson (1924)

"I have a terrific headache."

—Franklin Delano Roosevelt (1945)

"That's obvious."

**—John F. Kennedy, when told by Mrs. John Connally,
"You can't say that Dallas doesn't love you." (1963)**

SUCH SWEET SORROW

"Parting is all we know of heaven and all we need to know of hell."

—Emily Dickinson

AH ONE, AH TWO...PART TWO

"It's easy to play any musical instrument: all you have to do is touch the right key at the right time, and the instrument will play itself."

—J. S. Bach

"He who sings scares away his woes."

—Cervantes

"There are more love songs than anything else. If songs could make you do something, we'd all love one another."

—Frank Zappa

"Music is the mediator between the spiritual and the sensual life."

—Ludwig van Beethoven

"Extraordinary how potent cheap music is."

—Noël Coward

"After silence, that which comes nearest to expressing the inexpressible is music."

—Aldous Huxley

A SEWING POEM

Ah deary me! what needles!—well really I must say,
All things are sadly altered—(for the worse too)
since my day!
The pins have neither heads nor points—
the needles have no eyes,
And there's ne'er a pair of scissors
of the good old-fashioned size!
The very bodkins now are made in fine new-fangled ways,
And the good old British thimble—is a dream of other days!

—Lady Dufferin

QUOTES, WITH APPLIANCES

"Magnetism, as you recall from physics class, is a powerful force that causes certain items to be attracted to refrigerators."

—Dave Barry

"I have the body of an eighteen-year-old. I keep it in the fridge."

—Spike Milligan

"When you hunt animals, you may succeed or not. But when you open the fridge, you will succeed a hundred percent of the time."

—Nora Volkow

"I put instant coffee in a microwave oven and almost went back in time."

—Steven Wright

"Leftovers in their less visible form are called memories. Stored in the refrigerator of the mind and the cupboard of the heart."

—Thomas Fuller

"I want to get a job as someone who names kitchen appliances. Toaster, refrigerator, blender…all you do is say what the sh*t does, and add 'er.' I wanna work for the Kitchen Appliance Naming Institute. Hey, what does that do? It keeps sh*t fresh. Well, that's a fresher. I'm going on break."

—**Mitch Hedberg**

"Everyone is kneaded out of the same dough but not baked in the same oven."

—**Yiddish proverb**

"Nature abhors a vacuum."

—**François Rabelais**

SHAKE IT UP BABY

"When liberty comes with hands dabbled in blood, it is hard to shake hands with her."

—**Oscar Wilde**

"First I shake the whole tree, that the ripest might fall. Then I climb the tree and shake each limb, and then each branch and then each twig, and then I look under each leaf."

—**Martin Luther**

"Sometimes I want to clean up my desk and go out and say, Respect me, I'm a respectable grown-up, and other times I just want to jump into a paper bag and shake and bake myself to death."

—**Wendy Wasserstein**

"Reason is a very light rider, and easily shook off."

—**Jonathan Swift**

SMART MOUTH: LINUS PAULING

"If you want to have good ideas, you must have many ideas. Most of them will be wrong, and what you have to learn is which ones to throw away."

"Your elder, no matter whether he has gray hair, no matter whether he is a Nobel laureate, may be wrong."

"I have something that I call my Golden Rule. It goes like this: 'Do unto others twenty-five percent better than you expect them to do unto you.' The twenty-five percent is for error."

"Do not let medical authorities or politicians mislead you. Find out what the facts are, and make your own decisions about how to live a happy life and how to work for a better world."

"Satisfying one's curiosity is one of the greatest sources of happiness in life."

"It no longer makes sense to kill twenty million or forty million people because of a dispute between two nations who are running things, or decisions made by the people who really are running things. Nobody wins."

"Science will go on. More interesting discoveries will be made that I have not the imagination to describe and I am awaiting them, full of curiosity and enthusiasm."

HMMM...

"If a goat could lower his tail, his ass wouldn't shine."

—Anonymous

SO?

"As my father always used to tell me, 'You see, son, there's always someone in the world worse off than you.' And I always used to think, 'So?'"

—Bill Bryson

ON FOOTBALL

"You have to play this game like somebody just hit your mother with a two-by-four."

—Dan Birdwell

"Football is, after all, a wonderful way to get rid of your aggressions without going to jail for it."

—Heywood Hale Broun

"When I played pro football, I never set out to hurt anyone deliberately—unless it was, you know, important, like a league game or something."

—Dick Butkus

"Kicking is very important in football. In fact, some of the more enthusiastic players even kick the ball, occasionally."

—Alfred Hitchcock

"I do not like football, which I think of as a game in which two tractors approach each other from opposite directions and collide. Besides, I have contempt for a game in which players have to wear so much equipment. Men play basketball in their underwear, which seems just right to me."

—Anna Quindlen

BODY BLOW

"The spine is man's Achilles' heel."

—Andre Brie

INSULTS, FROM SHAKESPEARE

"You scullion! You rampallian! You fustilarian! I'll tickle your catastrophe!"

—*Henry IV, Part 2*

"Methink'st thou art a general offence and every man should beat thee."

—*All's Well That Ends Well*

"Go, prick thy face, and over-red thy fear, Thou lily-liver'd boy."

—*Macbeth*

"A knave, a rascal, an eater of broken meats; a base, proud, shallow, beggarly, three-suited, hundred-pound, filthy worsted-stocking knave; a lily-livered, action-taking, glass-gazing, super-serviceable, finical rogue; one-trunk-inheriting slave; one that art nothing but the composition of a knave, beggar, coward, pander, and the son and heir to a mongrel bitch: one whom I will beat into clamorous whining if thou deni'st the least syllable of thy addition."

—*King Lear*

"He's a disease that must be cut away."

—*Coriolanus*

"Thou clay-brained guts, thou knotty-pated fool, thou whoreson obscene greasy tallow-catch!"

—*Henry IV, Part 1*

"Thy tongue outvenoms all the worms of Nile."

—*Cymbeline*

"Thou art a flesh-monger, a fool and a coward."

—*Measure for Measure*

"It is certain that when he makes water, his urine is congealed ice."

—*Measure for Measure*

"I do wish thou wert a dog, That I might love thee something."

—*Timon of Athens*

SHHH...

"The inability to stay quiet is one of the conspicuous failings of mankind."

—Walter Bagehot

"He who establishes his argument by noise and command shows that his reason is weak."

—Michel de Montaigne

"Cultivate quietness in your speech, in your thoughts, in your emotions. Speak habitually low. Wait for attention and then your low words will be charged with dynamite."

—Elbert Hubbard

"Noise proves nothing. Often a hen who has merely laid an egg cackles as if she laid an asteroid."

—Mark Twain

"Silence is the true friend that never betrays."

—Confucius

"Four-fifths of all our troubles would disappear if we would only sit down and keep still."

—Calvin Coolidge

"It's so simple to be wise. Just think of something stupid to say, and then don't say it."

—Sam Levenson

A LITTLE BIT LOUDER NOW

"Sing out loud in the car, even—or especially—if it embarrasses your children."

—Marilyn Penland

A LITTLE BIT CHOWDER NOW

"Fishiest of all places was the Try Pots, which well deserved its name; for the pots there were always boiling chowders. Chowder for breakfast, and chowder for dinner, and chowder for supper, till you began to look for fish-bones coming through your clothes."

—Herman Melville, *Moby-Dick*

MORE RANDOM WISDOM

"Out beyond ideas of wrongdoing and right-doing, there is a field. I will meet you there."

—Rumi

"We are what we pretend to be. So we must be careful what we pretend to be."

—Kurt Vonnegut

"The optimist proclaims that we live in the best of all possible worlds, and the pessimist fears this is true."

—James Branch Cabell

"Both optimists and pessimists contribute to our society. The optimist invents the airplane, and the pessimist the parachute."

—Gil Stern

"If a problem has no solution, it may not be a problem, but a fact—not to be solved, but to be coped with."

—Shimon Peres

TWO KINDS OF ARTISTS

"There are two kinds of artists left: those who endorse Pepsi and those who simply won't."

—Annie Lennox

SPOUTING OFF

"Cetaceans seem to spend an inordinate amount of time in sexual activity. This may be generated by boredom in captivity, but observers in the wild tend to confirm it. Dolphins engage in love-play with almost every creature in sight—with mothers, brothers, fathers, daughters, cousins or aunts. There is even one record of a bottlenose dolphin masturbating with a herring."

—Robin Brown, *The Lure of the Dolphin*

SMART MOUTH: FEDERICO FELLINI

"Nietzsche claimed that his genius was in his nostrils, and I think that is a very excellent place for it to be."

"A different language is a different vision of life."

"Money is everywhere, but so is poetry. What we lack are the poets."

"Everyone knows that time is Death, that Death hides in clocks. Imposing another time powered by the Clock of the Imagination, however, can refuse his law. Here, freed of the Grim Reaper's scythe, we learn that pain is knowledge and all knowledge pain."

"Going to the cinema is like returning to the womb; you sit there, still and meditative in the darkness, waiting for life to appear on the screen."

DON'T!

"Don't go backwards; you have already been there."

—Ray Charles

"Don't think. Thinking is the enemy of creativity. It's self-conscious, and anything self-conscious is lousy. You can't try to do things. You simply must do things."

—Ray Bradbury

"Don't overestimate the decency of the human race."

—H. L. Mencken

"Don't let yesterday use up too much of today."

—Will Rogers

"Don't listen to friends when the friend inside you says, 'Do this.'"

—Mohandas K. Gandhi

"Don't ever take a fence down until you know why it was put up."

—Robert Frost

"Don't confuse fame with success. Madonna is one; Helen Keller is the other."

—Erma Bombeck

HMMM...

"I'm addicted to placebos. I'd give them up, but it wouldn't make any difference."

—Jay Leno

RETURN OF THE CAT IN THE QUOTE

"The cat could very well be man's best friend but would never stoop to admitting it."

—Doug Larson

"When I play with my cat, who knows whether she is not amusing herself with me more than I with her."

—Michel de Montaigne

"If man could be crossed with the cat, it would improve man but deteriorate the cat."

—Mark Twain

"A dog, I have always said, is prose; a cat is a poem."

—Jean Burden

"A cat's got her own opinion of human beings. She don't say much, but you can tell enough to make you anxious not to hear the whole of it."

—Jerome K. Jerome

DIAMOND MINDS

"Tom Seaver's so good that blind people come to the park just to hear him pitch."

—Reggie Jackson

"I'm beginning to see Brooks Robinson in my sleep. If I dropped this paper plate, he'd pick it up on the hop and throw me out at first."

—Sparky Anderson

"Cool Papa Bell was so fast he could turn out the light and jump in bed before the room got dark."

—Satchel Paige

"Rod Carew's the only guy I know who can go 4-for-3."

—Alan Bannister

"[Babe Ruth] hit 'em so high that everyone on the field thought he had a chance to get it. They'd all try to get under it to make the catch, and it looked like a union meeting."

—Casey Stengel

"Lou Gehrig never learned that a ballplayer couldn't be good every day."

—Hank Gowdy

"What's the best way to pitch to Stan Musial? That's easy. Walk him and then try to pick him off first base."

—Joe Garagiola

"The only thing Cy Young didn't win was the Cy Young Award."

—Joe Torre

QUOTES, WITH SUBMARINES

"I must confess that my imagination refuses to see any sort of submarine doing anything but suffocating its crew and floundering at sea."

—H. G. Wells

"In the long course of history, having people who understand your thought is much greater security than another submarine."

—J. William Fulbright

"The question of whether computers can think is just like the question of whether submarines can swim."

—Edsger W. Dijkstra

Ringo: "Hey, would you believe me if I told you I was being followed by a yellow submarine?"
Police officer: "No, no, I would not."
Ringo: "Oh, yeah, didn't think you would. I could've sworn I saw a yellow submarine. But that's not logic now, is it? It must've been one of them 'Unidentified Flying Cupcakes.'"

—*Yellow Submarine* (1968)

THIRTEEN EPITAPHS

There Goes the Neighborhood.

—Rodney Dangerfield

The greatest honor history can bestow
is the title of peacemaker.

—Richard M. Nixon

One Heart and One Soul.

—John Candy

Together Again.

—George Burns and Gracie Allen

And the Beat Goes On.

—Sonny Bono

Thank you for the many beautiful songs.
They will live long and longer.

—Hank Williams

An American soldier and
defender of the Constitution.

—Jefferson Davis

Sleep after toil,
port after stormy seas,
ease after war,
death after life,
does greatly please.

—Joseph Conrad

The passive master lent his hand,
to the vast soul which o'er him planned.

—Ralph Waldo Emerson

Called back.

—Emily Dickinson

Steel true, blade straight.

—Sir Arthur Conan Doyle

Don't try.

—Charles Bukowski

That nothing's so sacred as honor
and nothing's so loyal as love.

—Wyatt and Josephine Earp

Peace at last.

—Lenny Bruce

SMART MOUTH: NELSON MANDELA

"There is no such thing as part freedom; it is all or nothing."

"A good head and a good heart are always a formidable combination. But when you add to that a literate tongue or pen, then you have something very special."

"We must use time wisely and forever realize that the time is always ripe to do right."

"There can be no keener revelation of a society's soul than the way in which it treats its children."

"There is nothing like returning to a place that remains unchanged to find the ways in which you yourself have altered."

"True reconciliation does not consist in merely forgetting the past."

"If you talk to a man in a language he understands, that goes to his head. If you talk to him in his language, that goes to his heart."

"As we are liberated from our own fear, our presence automatically liberates others."

"Money won't create success; the freedom to make it will."

"And as we let our own light shine, we unconsciously give other people permission to do the same."

"After climbing a great hill, one only finds that there are many more hills to climb."

"It always seems impossible until it's done."

SHADOWS AND LIGHT

"Things are as they are. Looking out into the universe at night, we make no comparisons between right and wrong stars, nor between well and badly arranged constellations."

—Alan Watts

"I don't need a friend who changes when I change and who nods when I nod; my shadow does that much better."

—Plutarch

"You do not have to sit outside in the dark. If, however, you want to look at the stars, you will find that darkness is necessary. But the stars neither require nor demand it."

—Annie Dillard

"Light thinks it travels faster than anything but it is wrong. No matter how fast light travels, it finds the darkness has always got there first, and is waiting for it."

—Terry Pratchett

"Everyone is a moon, and has a dark side which he never shows to anybody."

—Mark Twain

ON FREEDOM

"They are not free who drag their chains after them."

—French proverb

CHAPTER 18

'TIL BACON DO US PART

"In a meal of bacon and eggs, the chicken is involved—the pig is committed."

—Richard Pratt

THREE FOR THROBBING

"The heart is pure theater throbbing in its cage palpably as any nightingale."

—Dr. Richard Selzer

"Develop an interest in life as you see it; the people, things, literature, music—the world is so rich, simply throbbing with rich treasures, beautiful souls and interesting people. Forget yourself."

—Henry Miller

"Leisure time should be an occasion for deep purpose to throb and for ideas to ferment. Where a man allows leisure to slip without some creative use, he has forfeited a bit of happiness."

—C. Neil Strait

SMART MOUTH: LUCILLE BALL

"What could I do? I couldn't dance. I couldn't sing. I could *talk*."

"Women's lib? It doesn't interest me one bit. I've been so liberated it hurts."

"How was *I Love Lucy* born? We decided that instead of divorce lawyers profiting from our mistakes, we'd profit from them."

"A man who correctly guesses a woman's age may be smart, but he's not very bright."

"I suppose I've grown old gracefully—'gracefully' meaning I've stemmed the tide. But there's a leak in the dike."

"Love yourself first, and everything else falls into line. You really have to love yourself to get anything done in this world."

THE SAVAGE GARDEN

"In spite of all the refinements of society that conspired to make art—the dizzying perfection of the string quartet or the sprawling grandeur of Fragonard's canvases—beauty was savage. It was as dangerous and lawless as the earth had been eons before man had one single coherent thought in his head or wrote codes of conduct on tablets of clay. Beauty was a Savage Garden."

—Anne Rice

A QUESTION OF FAITH

"To suppose that the eye with all its inimitable contrivances for adjusting the focus to different distances, for admitting different amounts of light, and for the correction of spherical and chromatic aberration, could have been formed by natural selection, seems, I confess, absurd in the highest degree."

—Charles Darwin

ON RELIGION

"Religion today is not transforming people; rather it is being transformed by the people. It is not raising the moral level of society; it is descending to society's own level, and congratulating itself that it has scored a victory because society is smilingly accepting its surrender."

—A. W. Tozer

"Faith is believing what you know ain't so."

—Mark Twain

"To surrender to ignorance and call it God has always been premature, and it remains premature today."

—Isaac Asimov

"A friendly study of the world's religions is a sacred duty."

—Mohandas K. Gandhi

"Religion altars the mind."

—Tony Follari

THREE EULOGIES

"He had a natural reserve to him, but when he admired people, he went all out to tell them about it. And because there was no deception in him, his praise meant more than just about anything else. If Chet was a fan of yours, you never needed another one. He was not a saint. He liked synthesizers more than he maybe ought to have. He sometimes kicked the golf ball to improve his lie."

—Garrison Keillor, on guitarist Chet Atkins

"He was a Dostoevsky, a Melville, and a Tolstoy all rolled up in one. He was an uncompromising giant unafraid to tackle controversial issues and explore the human condition through his unique vision."

—Edward Champion, on Stanley Kubrick

"Here lies the body of my good horse, 'The General.' For twenty years he bore me around the circuit of my practice, and in all that time he never made a blunder. Would that his master could say the same!"

—President John Tyler, on "The General"

MORE QUOTATIONS COURAGEOUS

"What makes the elephant charge his tusk in the misty mist, or the dusky dusk? What makes the muskrat guard his musk? Courage!"

—The Cowardly Lion (Bert Lahr), *The Wizard of Oz* (1939)

"The man who knows when not to act is wise. To my mind, bravery is forethought."

—Euripides

"Courage is not the absence of fear, but rather the judgment that something else is more important than fear."

—Ambrose Redmoon

"It is curious—curious that physical courage should be so common in the world, and moral courage so rare."

—Mark Twain

"Courage is the power to overcome danger, misfortune, fear, injustice, while continuing to affirm inwardly that life with all its sorrows is good; that everything is meaningful even if in a sense beyond our understanding; and that there is always tomorrow."

—Dorothy Thompson

NEVER!

"Never exaggerate your faults; your friends will attend to that."

—Robert C. Edwards

"Never help a child with a task at which he feels he can succeed."

—Maria Montessori

"Never insult anyone by accident."

—Robert A. Heinlein

"Never believe anything in politics until it has been officially denied."

—Otto von Bismarck

"Never play a thing the same way twice."

—Louis Armstrong

"Never invest your money in anything that eats or needs repairing.

—Billy Rose

"Never mind your happiness; do your duty."

—Will Durant

"Never under any circumstances take a sleeping pill and a laxative on the same night."

—Dave Barry

ON THE ROAD, AGAIN

"When preparing to travel, lay out all your clothes and all your money. Then take half the clothes and twice the money."

—Susan Heller

"Thanks to the Interstate Highway System, it is now possible to travel across the country from coast to coast without seeing anything."

—Charles Kuralt

"Wandering reestablishes the original harmony which once existed between man and the universe."

—Anatole France

"The traveler was active; he went strenuously in search of people, of adventure, of experience. The tourist is passive; he expects interesting things to happen to him. He goes 'sight-seeing.'"

—**Daniel J. Boorstin**

"There are only two emotions in a plane: boredom and terror."

—**Orson Welles**

"I dislike feeling at home when I am abroad."

—**George Bernard Shaw**

"Traveling is like flirting with life. It's like saying, 'I would stay and love you, but I have to go; this is my station.'"

—**Lisa St. Aubin de Teran**

NIGHT MUSIC

"How lovely are the portals of the night,
When stars come out to watch the daylight die."

—**Thomas Cole**

"There they stand, the innumerable stars, shining in order like a living hymn, written in light."

—**N. P. Willis**

"Twilight drops her curtain down, and pins it with a star."

—**Lucy Maud Montgomery**

"Night's black Mantle covers all alike."

—**Guillaume de Salluste du Bartas**

"With finger on her solemn lip,
Night hushed the shadowy earth."

—Margaret Deland

"The night walked down the sky with the moon in her hand."

—Frederick L. Knowles

"And the night shall be filled with music,
And the cares that infest the day
Shall fold their tents like the Arabs
And as silently steal away."

—Henry Wadsworth Longfellow

"There are nights when the wolves are silent and only the moon howls."

—George Carlin

"By night, an atheist half believes in God."

—Edward Young

ON ENGINEERS

"Normal people...believe that if it ain't broke, don't fix it.
Engineers believe that if it ain't broke, it doesn't have enough features yet."

—Scott Adams

"The great liability of the engineer compared to men of other professions is that his works are out in the open where all can see them. If his works do not work, he is damned. That is the phantasmagoria that haunts his nights and dogs his days."

—Herbert Hoover

"One has to look out for engineers—they begin with sewing machines and end up with the atomic bomb."

—Marcel Pagnol

"To define it rudely but not ineptly, engineering is the art of doing that well with one dollar which any bungler can do with two after a fashion."

—Arthur Wellesley

"Death and taxes are unsolved engineering problems."

—Romana Machado

"'*Via ovicpitum dura est*,' or, for the benefit of the engineers among you: 'The way of the egghead is hard.'"

—Adlai Stevenson

INSIDE OUT

"Life is a zoo in a jungle."

—Peter De Vries

JUNK IN A QUOTE

"My favorite review described me as the cinematic equivalent of junk mail."

—Steve Buscemi

"Rice Krispies happens to be one of my favorite junk foods, just as I regard Michener as superior among junk writers."

—Christopher Lehmann-Haupt

"A junky runs on junk time. When his junk is cut off, the clock runs down and stops. All he can do is hang on and wait for non-junk time to start."

—William S. Burroughs

"Junk journalism is the evidence of a society that has got at least one thing right, that there should be nobody with the power to dictate where responsible journalism begins."

—Tom Stoppard

"Democracy with its semi-civilization sincerely cherishes junk. The artist's power should be spiritual. But the power of the majority is material. When these worlds meet occasionally, it is pure coincidence."

—Paul Klee

CITIES OF THE WORLD

"There is a story that when incoming jets throttle back for the approach to Belfast's Aldergrove Airport, the pilots tell their passengers to put their watches back to local time—1690."

—Russell Miller

"The great thing about Glasgow is that if there's a nuclear attack it'll look exactly the same afterwards."

—Billy Connolly

"Liverpool can be very lonely on a Saturday night, and it's only Thursday morning."

—Paul Angelis

"Amsterdam did not answer our expectations; it is a kind of paltry, rubbishy Venice."

—**William Hazlitt**

"Paris is always Paris and Berlin is never Berlin!"

—**Jack Lang**

"Prague is like a vertical Venice—steps everywhere."

—**Penelope Gilliatt**

"*On the Beach* is a story about the end of the world, and Melbourne sure is the right place to film it."

—**Ava Gardner**

"San Francisco itself is art, above all literary art. Every block is a short story, every hill a novel. Every home a poem, every dweller within immortal. That is the whole truth."

—**William Saroyan**

"If the Mafia exists in Montreal, it's probably like the Knights of Columbus."

—**Armand Courville**

SWIMMING UPSTREAM

"The preternaturally early bird in his greedy haste may catch the worm; but the salmon never take the fly until the fog has lifted; and in this the scientific angler sees, with gratitude, a remarkable adaptation of the laws of nature to the tastes of man."

—**Henry Van Dyke**

"But Loki did not escape his deserved punishment…Odin found out his hiding-place and the gods assembled to take him. He, seeing this, changed himself into a salmon, and lay hid among the stones of the brook. But the gods took his net and dragged the brook, and Loki, finding he must be caught, tried to leap over the net; but Thor caught him by the tail and compressed it, so that salmons ever since have had that part remarkably fine and thin."

**—Thomas Bulfinch,
on Norse mythology**

"When you feel neglected, think of the female salmon, who lays 3,000,000 eggs but no one remembers her on Mother's Day."

—Sam Ewing

WHO'S IN CHARGE?

"He that cannot obey, cannot command."

—Benjamin Franklin

"The one who loves the least controls the relationship."

—Robert Anthony

"Worker bees can leave. Even drones can fly away. The queen is their slave."

—Chuck Palahniuk

"The belly is the commanding part of the body."

—Homer

NA ZDOROVJE!

There cannot be not enough snacks,
There can only be not enough vodka.
There can be no silly jokes,
There can only be not enough vodka.
There can be no ugly women,
There can only be not enough vodka.
There cannot be too much vodka,
There can only be not enough vodka.

—Russian drinking song

GENE ON WOODY

"Woody [Allen] makes a movie as if he were lighting 10,000 safety matches to illuminate a city. Each one is a little epiphany: topical, ethnic, or political."

—Gene Wilder

SMART MOUTH: DAME EDITH SITWELL

"I have often wished I had time to cultivate modesty. But I am too busy thinking about myself."

"I am patient with stupidity, but not with those who are proud of it."

"The poet speaks to all men of that other life of theirs that they have smothered and forgotten."

"I'm not the man to balk at a low smell, I not the man to insist on asphodel. This sounds like a He-fellow, don't you think? It sounds like that. I belch, I bawl, I drink."

"Good taste is the worst vice ever invented."

"Still falls the rain—dark as the world of man, black as our loss—
blind as the nineteen hundred and forty nails upon the Cross."

"Vulgarity is, in reality, nothing but a modern, chic, pert descendant of the goddess Dullness."

> Each dull wooden stalactite
> Of rain creaks, hardened by the light
> Sounding like an overtone
> From some lonely world unknown.

MONKEYSHINES

"Trouble came—as trouble so often does—with a monkey."

—Paul Collins

"An American monkey, after getting drunk on brandy, would never touch it again, and thus is much wiser than most men."

—Charles Darwin

"Artistic genius is an expansion of monkey imitativeness."

—Winwood W. Reade

"Some determined advocates of the vegetable system maintain that the teeth and stomach of the monkey correspond, in structure, very closely with that of man, yet it lives on fruits—therefore if man followed nature, he would live on fruits and vegetables. But though the anatomical likeness between man and monkeys is striking, yet it is not complete; the difference may be and doubtless is precisely that which makes a difference of diet necessary to nourish and develop their dissimilar natures. Those who should live as the monkeys do would most closely resemble them."

—Sarah Josepha Hale

"When the monkey can't reach the ripe banana with his hand, he says it is not sweet."

—Sudanese proverb

"Monkeys are superior to men in this: when a monkey looks into a mirror, he sees a monkey."

—Malcolm De Chazal

"I think the monkeys at the zoo should have to wear sunglasses so they can't hypnotize you."

—Jack Handey

"The surest way to make a monkey of a man is to quote him."

—Robert Benchley

IN THE GARDEN

"A garden is the best alternative therapy."

—Germaine Greer

"Gardening requires lots of water—most of it in the form of perspiration."

—Lou Erickson

"A garden is always a series of losses set against a few triumphs, like life itself."

—May Sarton

"Your first job is to prepare the soil. The best tool for this is your neighbor's garden tiller. If your neighbor does not own a garden tiller, suggest that he buy one."

—Dave Barry

"What a man needs in gardening is a cast-iron back, with a hinge in it."

—Charles Dudley Warner

"The best place to seek God is in a garden. You can dig for him there."

—George Bernard Shaw

"In gardens, beauty is a by-product. The main business is sex and death."

—Sam Llewelyn

"Gardening is a kind of disease. It infects you, you cannot escape it. When you go visiting, your eyes rove about the garden; you interrupt the serious cocktail drinking because of an irresistible impulse to get up and pull a weed."

—Lewis Gannit

"Para-science tells us that geraniums bloom better if they are spoken to. But a kind word every now and then is really quite enough. Too much attention, like too much feeding, and weeding and hoeing, inhibits and embarrasses them."

—Victoria Glendinning

"Last night, there came a frost, which has done great damage to my garden....It is sad that Nature will play such tricks on us poor mortals, inviting us with sunny smiles to confide in her, and then, when we are entirely within her power, striking us to the heart."

—Nathaniel Hawthorne

"Weather means more when you have a garden. There's nothing like listening to a shower and thinking how it is soaking in around your green beans."

—Marcelene Cox

"Unemployment is capitalism's way of getting you to plant a garden."

—Orson Scott Card

"Coffee. Garden. Coffee. Does a good morning need anything else?"

—Betsy Cañas Garmon

"All gardeners live in beautiful places because they make them so."

—Joseph Joubert

"In the spring, at the end of the day, you should smell like dirt."

—Margaret Atwood

HOW'S THE WEATHER?

"Sunshine is delicious, rain is refreshing, wind braces us up, snow is exhilarating; there is really no such thing as bad weather, only different kinds of good weather."

—John Ruskin

CHAPTER 19

FACEOFF

"No man, for any considerable period, can wear one face to himself, and another to the multitude, without finally getting bewildered as to which may be true."

—Nathaniel Hawthorne

ON THE INTERNET

"I must confess that I've never trusted the Web. I've always seen it as a coward's tool. Where does it live? How do you hold it personally responsible? Can you put a distributed network of fiber-optic cable 'on notice'? And is it male or female? In other words, can I challenge it to a fight?"

—Stephen Colbert

"The Internet is the first thing that humanity has built that humanity doesn't understand, the largest experiment in anarchy that we have ever had."

—Eric Schmidt

"The Internet is so big, so powerful and pointless that for some people it is a complete substitute for life."

—Andrew Brown

"The Internet is a telephone system that's gotten uppity."

—Clifford Stoll

GOLDEN SLUMBERS

"The bed is a bundle of paradoxes: we go to it with reluctance, yet we quit it with regret; we make up our minds every night to leave it early, but we make up our bodies every morning to keep it late."

—Charles Caleb Colton

"Sleep opens within us an inn for phantoms. In the morning we must sweep out the shadows."

—Gaston Bachelard

"It is a common experience that a problem difficult at night is resolved in the morning after the committee of sleep has worked on it."

—John Steinbeck

"Sleeplessness is a desert without vegetation or inhabitants."

—Jessamyn West

"Sleep is the interest we have to pay on the capital which is called in at death; and the higher the rate of interest and the more regularly it is paid, the further the date of redemption is postponed."

—Arthur Schopenhauer

"There are twelve hours in the day, and above fifty in the night."

—Marie de Rabutin-Chantal

IN YOUR DREAMS

"Dreams are free therapy. Consult your inner Freud."

—Grey Livingston

"All dreams spin out from the same web."

—Hopi proverb

"Dreaming is an act of pure imagination, attesting in all men a creative power, which if it were available in waking, would make every man a Dante or Shakespeare."

—H. F. Hedge

"Dreams are excursions into the limbo of things, a deliverance from the human prison."

—Henri-Frédéric Amiel

"All the things one has forgotten scream for help in dreams."

—Elias Canetti

"Dreams say what they mean, but they don't say it in daytime language."

—Gail Godwin

"I think we dream so we don't have to be apart so long. If we're in each other's dreams, we can be together all the time."

—Hobbes (of *Calvin and Hobbes*)

A GOOD QUOTATION

"A good quotation gets out the mental screwdriver and adjusts the setscrew."

—Joan Larsen

SMART MOUTH:
WILLIAM SHAKESPEARE

"Love all, trust few. Do wrong to none."

—*All's Well That Ends Well*

"We are such stuff as dreams are made on, rounded with a little sleep."

—*The Tempest*

"Everyone can master a grief but he that has it."

—*Much Ado About Nothing*

"Have more than thou showest, speak less than thou knowest, lend less than thou owest."

—*King Lear*

"Some rise by sin, and some by virtue fall."

—*Measure for Measure*

"Speak low if you speak love."

—*Much Ado About Nothing*

"Cowards die many times before their deaths; The valiant never taste of death but once."

—Julius Caesar

"Love sought is good, but given unsought is better."

—Twelfth Night

ON CANCER

"Cancer patients are lied to, not just because the disease is (or is thought to be) a death sentence, but because it is felt to be obscene—in the original meaning of that word: ill-omened, abominable, repugnant to the senses."

—Susan Sontag

"My veins are filled, once a week with a Neapolitan carpet cleaner distilled from the Adriatic, and I am as bald as an egg. However, I still get around and am mean to cats."

—John Cheever

"It is in moments of illness that we are compelled to recognize that we live not alone but chained to a creature of a different kingdom, whole worlds apart, who has no knowledge of us and by whom it is impossible to make ourselves understood: our body."

—Marcel Proust

"We 'need' cancer because, by the very fact of its incurability, it makes all other diseases, however virulent, not cancer."

—Gilbert Adair

OLD

Lone and forgotten
through a long sleeping,
in the heart of age
a child woke weeping.
No invisible mother
was nigh him there
laughing and nodding
from earth and air.
No elfin comrades
came at his call
and the earth and the air
were blank as a wall.
The darkness thickened
upon him creeping,
in the heart of age
a child lay weeping.

—George William Russell

SMART MOUTH: LOU HOLTZ

"If you burn your neighbor's house down, it doesn't make your house look any better."

"You're never as good as everyone tells you when you win, and you're never as bad as they say when you lose."

"No one has ever drowned in sweat."

"You'll never get ahead of anyone as long as you try to get even with him."

"There's nothing is this world more instinctively abhorrent to me than finding myself in agreement with my fellow humans."

"When all is said and done, more is said than done."

ARCHAEOLOGY

"Archaeology is the Peeping Tom of the sciences. It is the sandbox of men who care not where they are going; they merely want to know where everyone else has been."

—Jim Bishop

"They always find in archaeology 'a series of small walls.' Every time, a series of small walls. Everywhere you go. 'We've found a series of small walls, we're very excited. I think this proves they had walls in olden days. They were very small, and... a series of small wall people.'"

—Eddie Izzard

"I married an archaeologist because the older I grow, the more he appreciates me."

—Agatha Christie

"Historians and archaeologists will one day discover that the ads of our time are the richest and most faithful reflections that any society ever made of its entire range of activities."

—Marshall McLuhan

"Yesterday in Egypt, archaeologists discovered the burial site for the fifty children of Ramses II. Fifty children! What I want to know is, who decided to name a condom after this guy?"

—Conan O'Brien

"An archaeologist is someone whose career lies in ruins."

—**Anonymous**

BASEBALL ON VALIUM

"The English are not very spiritual people, so they invented cricket to give them some idea of eternity."

—**George Bernard Shaw**

"Of course it's frightfully dull! That's the whole point! Any game can be exciting—football, dirt track racing, roulette...To go to cricket to be thrilled is as stupid as to go to a Chekhov play in search of melodrama."

—**Terence Rattigan**

"Many Continentals think life is a game; the English think cricket is a game."

—**George Mikes**

"Cricket makes no sense to me. I find it beautiful to watch and I like that they break for tea. That is very cool, but I don't understand."

—**Jim Jarmusch**

"Cricket needs brightening up a bit. My solution is to let the players drink at the beginning of the game, not after. It always works in our picnic matches."

—**Paul Hogan**

"Cricket is like sex films —they relieve frustration and tension."

—**Linda Lovelace**

"If the French noblesse had been capable of playing cricket with their peasants, their châteaux would never have been burnt."

—**G. M. Trevelyan**

"Cricket is basically baseball on Valium."

—**Robin Williams**

BE COOL

"There is nothing more galling to angry people than the coolness of those on whom they wish to vent their spleen."

—**Alexandre Dumas**

STEAL THESE QUOTES

"It has come to be practically a sort of rule in literature, that a man, having once shown himself capable of original writing, is entitled thenceforth to steal from the writings of others at discretion."

—**Ralph Waldo Emerson**

"Immature poets imitate; mature poets steal."

—**T. S. Eliot**

"Self-plagiarism is style."

—**Alfred Hitchcock**

"If you steal from one author, it's plagiarism; if you steal from many, it's research."

—**Wilson Mizner**

"If I find in a book anything I can make use of, I take it gratefully. My plays are full of pillage of this kind."

—George Bernard Shaw

"Perish those who said our good things before we did."

—Aelius Donatus

I SEE LONDON...

"Brothers should pull up their pants. Some people might not want to see your underwear—I'm one of them."

—Barack Obama

PEOPLE WITH TALENT

"Great talents are the most lovely and often the most dangerous fruits on the tree of humanity. They hang upon the most slender twigs that are easily snapped off."

—Carl Jung

QUOTES, WITH KNEES

"The best academy—a mother's knee."

—James Russell Lowell

"A woman is as young as her knee."

—Mary Quant

"Have you noticed that whatever sport you're trying to learn, some earnest person is always telling you to keep your knees bent?"

—Dave Barry

"Facts are ventriloquists' dummies. Sitting on a wise man's knee they may be made to utter words of wisdom; elsewhere, they say nothing, or talk nonsense, or indulge in sheer diabolism."

—Aldous Huxley

"I seated ugliness on my knee, and almost immediately grew tired of it."

—Salvador Dalí

"I'm afraid I was very much the traditionalist. I went down on one knee and dictated a proposal which my secretary faxed over straight away."

—Stephen Fry

WORDS ON CANVAS

"How vain is painting, which is admired for reproducing the likeness of things whose originals are not admired."

—Blaise Pascal

"What a funny thing painting is. The abstract painters always insist on their connection with the visible reality, while the so-called figurative artists insist that what they really care about is the abstract qualities of life."

—Marlene Dumas

"I've been doing a lot of abstract painting lately, extremely abstract. No brush, no paint, no canvas, I just think about it."

—Steven Wright

"Look, it's my misery that I have to paint this kind of painting, it's your misery that you have to love it, and the price of the misery is thirteen hundred and fifty dollars."

—Mark Rothko

"Only when he no longer knows what he is doing does the painter do good things."

—Edgar Degas

"There is only one absinthe drinker, and that's the man who painted this idiotic picture."

—Thomas Couture, on Manet's *Absinthe Drinker*

AUSTRALIA

"AUSTRALIA, n. A country lying in the South Sea, whose industrial and commercial development has been unspeakably retarded by an unfortunate dispute among geographers as to whether it is a continent or an island."

—Ambrose Bierce

KANGAROO

"Her little loose hands, and dropping Victorian shoulders.
And then her great weight below the waist, her vast pale belly
With a thin young yellow little paw hanging out,
and straggle of a long thin ear, like ribbon,
Like a funny trimming to the middle of her belly, thin little
dangle of an immature paw, and one thin ear."

—D. H. Lawrence, from the poem "Kangaroo"

UNDER THE BIG TOP

"Even though they probably didn't know it at the time, circus performers were practicing physics and math. Yes, it's fun and colorful, but you're still learning. You're learning without even knowing you are."

—Brenda Lewis

"Now the freaks are on television, the freaks are in the movies. And it's no longer the sideshow, it's the whole show. The colorful circus and the clowns and the elephants, for all intents and purposes, are gone, and we're dealing only with the freaks."

—Jonathan Winters

"Clowns and elephants are the pegs on which the circus is hung."

—P. T. Barnum

"I remember in the circus learning that the clown was the prince, the high prince. I always thought that the high prince was the lion or the magician, but the clown is the most important."

—Roberto Benigni

"Whips and chains belong in the bedroom, not the circus."

—Amandah Povilitus

"Keep the circus going inside you, keep it going, don't take anything too seriously, it'll all work out in the end."

—David Niven

"Damn everything but the circus."

—Corita Kent

GOOD ADVICE

"A lot of people enjoy being dead. But they are not dead, really. They're just backing away from life. Reach out. Take a chance. Get hurt even. But play as well as you can. Go team, go! Give me an L. Give me an I. Give me a V. Give me an E. L-I-V-E. LIVE! Otherwise, you got nothing to talk about in the locker room."

—Maude (Ruth Gordon), *Harold and Maude* (1971)

MIRRORS

"The world is a looking-glass, and gives back to every man the reflection of his own face. Frown at it, and it will in turn look sourly upon you; laugh at it and with it, and it is a jolly kind companion."

—William Makepeace Thackeray

"Books are like a mirror. If an ass looks in, you can't expect an angel to look out."

—B. C. Forbes

"Poetry is a mirror which makes beautiful that which is distorted."

—Percy Bysshe Shelley

"Behavior is the mirror in which everyone shows their image."

—Johann Wolfgang von Goethe

"If you wish to avoid seeing a fool, you must first break your looking-glass."

—François Rabelais

"Not to go to the theater is like making one's toilet without a mirror."

—Arthur Schopenhauer

"You've never seen death? Look in the mirror every day and you will see it like bees working in a glass hive."

—Jean Cocteau

PASS IT ON

"A man makes no noise over a good deed, but passes onto another as a vine to bear grapes again in season."

—Marcus Aurelius

THE GUN DEBATE

"Why is it that, as a culture, we are more comfortable seeing two men holding guns than holding hands?"

—Ernest Gaines

"I believe everybody in the world should have guns. Citizens, after a shooting spree, they always want to take the guns away from the people who didn't do it. I sure as hell wouldn't want to live in a society where the only people allowed guns are the police and the military."

—Scott Adams

"Every gun that is made, every warship launched, every rocket fired, signifies in the final sense a theft from those who hunger and are not fed, those who are cold and are not clothed."

—Dwight D. Eisenhower

"If guns are outlawed, only the government will have guns. Only the police, the secret police, the military, the hired servants of our rulers. Only the government—and a few outlaws. I intend to be among the outlaws."

—Edward Abbey

"Guns don't kill people, people kill people, and monkeys do too (if they have a gun)."

—Eddie Izzard

WHO KNOWS?

who knows if the moon's
a balloon, coming out of a keen city
in the sky—filled with pretty people?

—E. E. Cummings

CHEER UP

"The walls we build around us to keep sadness out also keeps out the joy."

—Jim Rohn

NO, REALLY, CHEER UP

"Killing yourself is a major commitment, it takes a kind of courage. Most people just lead lives of cowardly desperation. It's kinda half suicide where you just dull yourself with substances."

—R. Crumb

"Maybe this world is another planet's Hell."

—Aldous Huxley

BETTER TO BURN OUT...

"I would rather be ashes than dust! I would rather that my spark should burn out in a brilliant blaze than it should be stifled by dry-rot. I would rather be a superb meteor, every atom of me in magnificent glow, than a sleepy and permanent planet. The function of man is to live, not to exist. I shall not waste my days trying to prolong them. I shall use my time."

—Jack London

SMART MOUTH: RALPH WALDO EMERSON

"However mean your life is, meet it and live it: do not shun it and call it hard names. Cultivate poverty like a garden herb, like sage. Do not trouble yourself much to get new things, whether clothes or friends. Things do not change, we change. Sell your clothes and keep your thoughts."

"People seem not to see that their opinion of the world is also a confession of their character."

"You cannot do a kindness too soon, for you never know how soon it will be too late."

"None of us will ever accomplish anything excellent or commanding except when he listens to the whisper which is heard by him alone."

"As if you could kill time without injuring eternity."

"Every man supposes himself not to be fully understood or appreciated."

"Foolish consistency is the hobgoblin of small minds."

"I once had a sparrow alight upon my shoulder for a moment, while I was hoeing in a village garden, and I felt that I was more distinguished by that circumstance that I should have been by any epaulet I could have worn."

"In what concerns you much, do not think that you have companions: know that you are alone in the world."

"Beware when the great God lets loose a thinker on this planet."

HOW TO LOOK LIKE A CHAMPION

"The vision of a champion is someone who is bent over, drenched in sweat, and the point of exhaustion, when no one else is watching."

—Anson Dorrance

LADIES FIRST

"The one thing I do not want to be called is First Lady. It sounds like a saddle horse."

—Jacqueline Kennedy

"Always be on time. Never try to make any personal engagements. Do as little talking as humanly possible. Never be disturbed by anything. Always do what you're told to do as quickly as possible. Remember to lean back in a parade, so that people can see your husband. Don't get too fat to ride three on a seat. Get out of the way as quickly as you're not needed."

—Eleanor Roosevelt

"My first job in all honesty is going to continue to be mom-in-chief. Making sure that in this transition, which will be even more of a transition for the girls...that they are settled and that they know they will continue to be the center of our universe."

—Michelle Obama

"Any lady who is First Lady likes being First Lady. I don't care what they say, they like it."

—Richard M. Nixon

"Women are being considered as candidates for vice president of the United States because it is the worst job in America. It's amazing that men will take it. A job with real power is First Lady. I'd be willing to run for that. As far as the men who are running for president are concerned, they aren't even people I would date."

—Nora Ephron

"Somewhere out in this audience may even be someone who will one day follow in my footsteps, and preside over the White House as the president's spouse. I wish him well."

—Barbara Bush

YOUTH IS WASTED ON THE PLASTIC?

"Could the young but realize how soon they will become mere walking bundles of habits, they would give more heed to their conduct while in the plastic state."

—William James

ON BEING A MODEL

"You know you've made it when you've been molded in miniature plastic. But you know what children do with Barbie dolls—it's a bit scary, actually."

—**Cate Blanchett**

THE WALK OF LIFE

"I have two doctors, my left leg and my right."

—**G. M. Trevelyan**

"Before supper take a little walk; after supper do the same."

—**Erasmus**

"Climb the mountains and get their good tidings. Nature's peace will flow into you as sunshine flows into trees. The winds will blow their freshness into you, and the storms their energy, while cares will drop off like falling leaves."

—**John Muir**

"It is good to collect things; it is better to take walks."

—**Anatole France**

GENIUS!

"Genius is sorrow's child."

—**John Adams**

"Genius, in one respect, is like gold; numbers of persons are constantly writing about both, who have neither."

—**Charles Caleb Colton**

"Genius is no respecter of time, trouble, money, or persons, the four things around which human affairs turn most persistently."

—Samuel Butler

"The thinking of a genius does not proceed logically. It leaps with great ellipses."

—Dorothy Thompson

"Beware of notions like genius; they are a sort of magic wand, and should be used sparingly by anybody who wants to see things clearly."

—José Ortega y Gasset

QUIT JONES'N

"Never keep up with the Joneses. Drag them down to your level."

—Quentin Crisp

WHAT IS IT GOOD FOR? (PART TWO)

"War is delightful to those who have not experienced it."

—Desiderius Erasmus

"War is a racket. It always has been. It is possibly the oldest, easily the most profitable, surely the most vicious."

—General Smedley Butler

"Two armies that fight each other is like one large army that commits suicide."

—Henri Barbusse

"The great error of nearly all studies of war has been to consider war as an episode in foreign policies, when it is an act of interior politics."

—Simone Weil

"Peace demands the most heroic labor and the most difficult sacrifice. It demands greater heroism than war."

—Thomas Merton

GRAY WITHOUT ENVY

"By common consent gray hairs are a crown of glory; the only object of respect that can never excite envy."

—George Bancroft

SMART MOUTH: ELLEN DEGENERES

"I'm on the patch right now. It releases small dosages of approval until I no longer crave it."

"I'm a godmother, that's a great thing to be, a godmother. She calls me god for short, that's cute, I taught her that."

"Our egos tell us we're the only ones that have any kind of feelings. We're the only ones with a relationship. We're the only ones with family. You know, I think that if you kill a spider, there is a relationship that you're ruining. There's a conversation going on outside with the other spiders. 'Did you hear about Chris?.... Killed, yeah....Sneaker. And now Stephanie has nine hundred babies to raise all alone. Well, she's got her legs full, I'll tell you that right now. Chris was so kind, wouldn't hurt a fly. It's just been tough for them lately. They just lost their web last week. Those humans think they're so smart. Let them try shooting silk out of their butt and see what they can make.'"

"Stuffed deer heads on walls are bad enough, but it's worse when they are wearing sunglasses and have streamers in their antlers because then you know they were enjoying themselves at a party when they were shot."

"The only thing that scares me more than space aliens is the idea that there aren't any space aliens. We can't be the best that creation has to offer. I pray we're not all there is. If so, we're in big trouble."

BOO

"I can look at the knot in a piece of wood until it frightens me."

—William Blake

FROM THE LOCAL BAR

"The church is near but the road is icy, the bar is far away but I will walk carefully."

—Russian proverb

"There is nothing which has yet been contrived by man, by which so much happiness is produced as by a good tavern."

—Samuel Johnson

"A bartender is a temporary pharmacist with a limited inventory."

—Anonymous

"Many a man who thinks to found a home discovers that he has merely opened a tavern for his friends."

—George Norman Douglas

"Karaoke bars combine two of the nation's greatest evils: people who shouldn't drink, and people who shouldn't sing."

—Tom Dreesen

"The hardest part about being a bartender is figuring out who is drunk and who is just stupid."

—Richard Braunstein

"By the time a bartender knows what drink a man will have before he orders, there is little else about him worth knowing."

—Don Marquis

MILKIN' IT

"I said to the wife, 'Guess what I heard in the pub? They reckon the milkman has made love to every woman in this road except one.' And she said, 'I'll bet it's that stuck-up Phyllis at number twenty-three.'"

—Max Kauffmann

WILD WORLD OF PROVERBS

"Don't bargain for fish that are still in the water."

—India

"If you call one wolf, you invite the pack."

—Bulgaria

"A kind word can attract even the snake from his nest."

—Saudi Arabia

"Use your enemy's hand to catch a snake."

—Iran

"You cannot prevent the birds of sorrow from flying over your head, but you can prevent them from building a nest in your hair."

—China

"Caution is not cowardice; even the ants march armed."

—Uganda

THE ETERNAL SEA

"The woods are never solitary—they are full of whispering, beckoning, friendly life. But the sea is a mighty soul, forever moaning of some great, unshareable sorrow, which shuts it up into itself for all eternity."

—Lucy Maud Montgomery

ON WINE

"Name me any liquid except our own blood that flows more intimately and incessantly through the labyrinth of symbols we have conceived to make our status as human beings, from the rudest peasant festival to the mystery of the Eucharist. To take wine into our mouths is to savor a droplet of the river of human history."

—Clifton Fadiman

"Winemaking is the world's second-oldest profession and, no doubt, it has eased the burden of the world's oldest."

—Tony Aspler

"Wine is a living liquid containing no preservatives. Its life cycle comprises youth, maturity, old age, and death. When not treated with reasonable respect it will sicken and die."

—Julia Child

"Wine is the flower in the buttonhole of life."

—Werumeus Buning

"Tonight I will make a tun of wine, Set myself up with two bowls of it; First I will divorce absolutely reason and religion, Then take to wife the daughter of the vine."

—Omar Khayyam

"Wine is the most civilized thing in the world."

—Ernest Hemingway

THREE FOR THREE

"For a man to write well, there are required three necessaries: to read the best authors, observe the best speakers, and much exercise of his own style."

—Ben Jonson

"There are three rules for writing a novel. Unfortunately, no one knows what they are."

—W. Somerset Maugham

"Three be the things I shall never attain: Envy, content, and sufficient champagne."

—Dorothy Parker

THE END, PART TWO

"Death is only an horizon, and an horizon is only the limit of our sight. Open our eyes to see more clearly."

—William Penn

"From my rotting body, flowers shall grow and I am in them and that is eternity."

—**Edvard Munch**

"All human things are subject to decay, and when fate summons, monarchs must obey."

—**John Dryden**

"I'm not afraid of death because I don't believe in it. It's just getting out of one car, and into another."

—**John Lennon**

"All our knowledge merely helps us to die a more painful death than animals that know nothing."

—**Maurice Maeterlinck**

"If my doctor told me I had only six minutes to live, I wouldn't brood. I'd just type a little faster."

—**Isaac Asimov**

HMMM...

"I wonder if illiterate people get the full effect of alphabet soup?"

—**Jerry Seinfeld**

SMART MOUTH: MOHANDAS K. GANDHI

"A no uttered from deepest conviction is better and greater than a yes merely uttered to please, or what is worse, to avoid trouble."

"An ounce of practice is worth more than a ton of preaching."

"I look only to the good qualities of men. Not being faultless myself, I won't presume to probe into the faults of others."

"Intolerance is itself a form of violence and an obstacle to the growth of a true democratic spirit."

"Humanity is an ocean; if a few drops of the ocean are dirty, the ocean does not become dirty."

"I do not want to foresee the future. I am concerned with taking care of the present."

"An error does not become truth by reason of multiplied propagation, nor does truth become error because nobody will see it."

"If patience is worth anything, it must endure to the end of time."

WATER MUSIC

"No man drowns if he perseveres in praying to God, and can swim."

—Russian proverb

"The water is your friend. You don't have to fight with water, just share the same spirit as the water, and it will help you move."

—Aleksandr Popov

"For myself, losing is not coming second. It's getting out of the water knowing you could have done better. For myself, I have won every race I've been in."

—Ian Thorpe

It was like passing a boundary to dive
Into the sun-filled water, brightly leafed
And limbed and lighted out from bank to bank.
That's how the stars shine during the day.

—Wallace Stevens

ON INTELLIGENCE

"Of work comes knowledge, of knowledge comes fruitful work; of the union of knowledge and work comes the development of intelligence."

—Vinoba Bhave

"Let us by wise and constitutional measures promote intelligence among the people as the best means of preserving our liberties."

—James Monroe

"What a distressing contrast there is between the radiant intelligence of the child and the feeble mentality of the average adult."

—Sigmund Freud

"You don't realize that you're intelligent until it gets you into trouble."

—James Baldwin

"Intelligence—yes, but of what kind and aim? There is the intelligence of Socrates, and the intelligence of a thief or a forger."

—Ralph Waldo Emerson

"Perhaps imagination is only intelligence having fun."

—**George Scialabra**

"There is no greater evidence of superior intelligence than to be surprised at nothing."

—**Josh Billings**

PRISON VS. SOCIETY

"To assert in any case that a man must be absolutely cut off from society because he is absolutely evil amounts to saying that society is absolutely good, and no-one in his right mind will believe this today."

—**Albert Camus**

MORE LOVE

"One of the best things about love—the feeling of being wrapped, like a gift, in understanding."

—**Anatole Broyard**

"You don't love because, you love despite; not for the virtues, but despite the faults."

—**William Faulkner**

"There is love, of course. And then there's life, its enemy."

—**Jean Anouilh**

"Love never dies a natural death. It dies because we don't know how to replenish its source."

—**Anaïs Nin**

"God knows I wanted love. But the moment I had to choose between the man I loved and my dresses, I chose the dresses."

—Coco Chanel

"Someday, after mastering the winds, the waves, the tides and gravity, we shall harness for God the energies of love, and then, for a second time in the history of the world, man will have discovered fire."

—Teilhard de Chardin

I hate the way you talk to me.
And the way you cut your hair.
I hate the way you drive my car.
I hate it when you stare.
I hate your big dumb combat boots.
And the way you read my mind.
I hate you so much it makes me sick
—it even makes me rhyme.
I hate the way you're always right.
I hate it when you lie.
I hate it when you make me laugh
—even worse when you make me cry.
I hate it that you're not around.
And the fact that you didn't call.
But mostly I hate the way I don't hate you
—not even close, not even a little bit, not any at all.

—Kat Stratford (Julia Stiles)
***10 Things I Hate About You* (1999)**

CHAPTER 21

OH, MAN

"I love the male body. It's better designed than the male mind."

—Andrea Newman

"Women are the most powerful magnet in the universe. And all men are cheap metal. And we all know where north is."

—Larry Miller

SMART MOUTH: CARL SAGAN

"Philosophers and scientists confidently offer up traits said to be uniquely human, and the monkeys and apes casually knock them down—toppling the pretension that humans constitute some sort of biological aristocracy among the beings on Earth."

"Finding the occasional straw of truth awash in a great ocean of confusion requires intelligence, vigilance, dedication, and courage. But if we don't practice these tough habits of thought, we cannot hope to solve the truly serious problems that face us—and we risk becoming a nation of suckers, up for grabs by the next charlatan who comes along."

"Science is a way of thinking much more than it is a body of knowledge."

"Except for children (who don't know enough not to ask the important questions), few of us spend time wondering why nature is the way it is."

"I would love to believe that when I die I will live again, that some thinking, feeling, remembering part of me will continue. But as much as I want to believe that, and despite the ancient and world-wide cultural traditions that assert an afterlife, I know of nothing to suggest that it is more than wishful thinking. The world is so exquisite with so much love and moral depth, that there is no reason to deceive ourselves with pretty stories for which there's little good evidence. Far better it seems to me, in our vulnerability, is to look death in the eye and to be grateful every day for the brief but magnificent opportunity that life provides."

TWO FOR TRYING

"If you hear a voice within you say 'You cannot paint,' then by all means paint, and that voice will be silenced."

—Vincent van Gogh

"All you umpires, back to the bleachers. Referees, hit the showers. It's my game. I pitch, I hit, I catch. I run the bases. At sunset, I've won or lost. At sunrise, I'm out again, giving it the old try."

—Ray Bradbury

THE OTHER POOL

"Dressing a pool player in a tuxedo is like putting whipped cream on a hot dog."

—Minnesota Fats

"The game of billiards has destroyed my naturally sweet disposition."

—Mark Twain

The billiard sharp who any one catches,
His doom's extremely hard
He's made to dwell
In a dungeon cell
On a spot that's always barred.
And there he plays extravagant matches
In fitless finger-stalls
On a cloth untrue
With a twisted cue
And elliptical billiard balls!

—Gilbert and Sullivan, *The Mikado*

"The poolhall's a great equalizer. In the poolhall, nobody cares how old you are, how young you are, what color your skin is or how much money you've got in your pocket…It's about how you move. And I remember this kid once who could move around a pool table like nobody had ever seen. I mean, hour after hour, rack after rack, his shots just went in. The cue was part of his arm and the balls had eyes. And the thing that made him so good was…He thought he could never miss. I know, 'cause that kid was me."

—Johnny Doyle (Mars Callahan), *Poolhall Junkies* (2002)

AGING

"My health is good; it's my age that's bad."

—Roy Acuff

"Wisdom doesn't automatically come with old age. Nothing does—except wrinkles. It's true, some wines improve with age. But only if the grapes were good in the first place."

—Abigail Van Buren

"It's a sobering thought: when Mozart was my age, he was dead for two years."

—Tom Lehrer

"There's one advantage to being 102. No peer pressure."

—Dennis Wolfberg

"The secret to longevity is to keep breathing."

—Sophie Tucker

"I love being a great-grandparent, but what I hate is being the mother of a grandparent."

—Janet Anderson

"The hands on my biological clock are giving me the finger."

—Wendy Liebman

"You know you're getting older when the candles cost more than the cake."

—Bob Hope

"It takes a long time to grow young."

—**Pablo Picasso**

BE LEAN

"Go without a coat when it's cold; find out what cold is. Go hungry; keep your existence lean. Wear away the fat, get down to the lean tissue and see what it's all about. The only time you define your character is when you go without."

—**Henry Rollins**

THE ZERO-PERCENT SOLUTION

"It is as impossible for man to demonstrate the existence of God as it would be for even Sherlock Holmes to demonstrate the existence of Arthur Conan Doyle."

—**Frederick Beuchner**

SMART MOUTH: BILL COSBY

"My childhood should have taught me lessons for my own fatherhood, but it didn't because parenting can only be learned by people who have no children."

"Poets have said that the reason to have children is to give yourself immortality. Immortality? Now that I have five children, my only hope is that they are all out of the house before I die."

"Is the glass half full or half empty? It depends on whether you're pouring or drinking."

"Humans are the only creatures on earth that allow their children to come back home."

"Women don't want to hear what you think. Women want to hear what they think in a deeper voice."

"It's more blessed to give than to receive. Especially kittens."

MARMALADE THOUGHTS

"Marmalade in the morning has the same effect on taste buds that a cold shower has on the body."

—Jeanine Larmoth

"I got the blues thinking of the future, so I left off and made some marmalade. It's amazing how it cheers one up to shred oranges and scrub the floor."

—D. H. Lawrence

The jelly—the jam and the marmalade,
And the cherry and quince "preserves" she made!
And the sweet-sour pickles of peach and pear,
With cinnamon in 'em, and all things rare!
And the more we ate was the more to spare,
Out to old Aunt Mary's! Ah!

—James Whitcomb Riley

HMMM...

"A Thaum is the basic unit of magical strength. It has been universally established as the amount of magic needed to create one small white pigeon or three normal-sized billiard balls."

—Terry Pratchett

TWELVE MORE EPITAPHS

So we beat on, boats against the current,
borne back ceaselessly into the past.

—F. Scott & Zelda Fitzgerald

Everybody Loves Somebody Sometime.

—Dean Martin

That's All folks.

—Mel Blanc

Workers of all lands unite. The philosophers
have only interpreted the world in various
ways; the point is to change it.

—Karl Marx

Nothing of him that doth fade
But doth suffer a sea-change
Into something rich and strange.

—Percy Bysshe Shelley

Cast a cold Eye
On life, on Death
Horseman, pass by.

—William Butler Yeats

I am ready to meet my Maker.
Whether my Maker is prepared for
the great ordeal of meeting me is another matter.

—Winston Churchill

I Had A Lover's Quarrel With The World.

—Robert Frost

Let the big guns boom over me.
—**Choctaw chief Pushmataha**

Murdered by a traitor and a coward
whose name is not worthy to appear here.
—**Jesse James**

Against you I will fling myself,
unvanquished and unyielding, O Death!

—**Virginia Woolf**

If you seek my monument,
look around you.

—**Christpoher Wren**

AH ONE, AH TWO...PART THREE

"It is cruel, you know, that music should be so beautiful. It has the beauty of loneliness of pain: of strength and freedom. The beauty of disappointment and never-satisfied love. The cruel beauty of nature and everlasting beauty of monotony."

—**Benjamin Britten**

"No good opera plot can be sensible, for people do not sing when they are feeling sensible."

—**W. H. Auden**

"Classical music is the kind we keep thinking will turn into a tune."

—**Kin Hubbard**

"Muzak goes in one ear...and out some other opening."

—**Anton Kuerti**

"It is a funny thing, but when I am making music, all the answers I seek for in life seem to be there, in the music. Or rather, I should say, when I am making music, there are no questions and no need for answers."

—Gustav Mahler

"I don't care if a dude is purple with green breath as long as he can swing."

—Miles Davis

"Making music should not be left to the professionals."

—Michelle Shocked

POOR OLD MUM

"My mom said she learned how to swim when someone took her out in the lake and threw her off the boat. I said, 'Mom, they weren't trying to teach you how to swim.'"

—Paula Poundstone

TRUST

"Trust only movement. Life happens at the level of events, not of words. Trust movement."

—Alfred Adler

"Where large sums of money are concerned, it is advisable to trust nobody."

—Agatha Christie

"I have great faith in fools—my friends call it self-confidence."

—Edgar Allan Poe

"Trust no one unless you have eaten much salt with him."

—Cicero

"The chief lesson I have learned in a long life is that the only way to make a man trustworthy is to trust him; and the surest way to make him untrustworthy is to distrust him and show your distrust."

—Henry L. Stimson

"He liked to fix things. One day he was repairing the light fixture above the face bowl in the bathroom. He asked me to hold one of his hands and to grip the faucet of the bathtub with my other hand. I did this. Then he licked the index finger of his free hand and stuck it up into the empty socket where the lightbulb had been. As the electricity passed through him and into me and through me and was grounded in the faucet of the bathtub, my father kept saying, 'Pal, I won't hurt you. I won't hurt you.' If I had let go of the faucet, both of us would have died. If I had let go of his hand, he would have died."

—James Alan McPherson

QUOTE THE RAVEN

"To the raven her own chick is white."

—Irish proverb

"He that visits the sick in hopes of a legacy, but is never so friendly in all other cases, I look upon him as being no better than a raven that watches a weak sheep only to peck out its eyes."

—Seneca

"Does wisdom perhaps appear on the earth as a raven which is inspired by the smell of carrion?"

—Friedrich Nietzsche

"Though thy crest be shorn and shaven, thou,"
I said, "art sure no craven,
Ghastly grim and ancient raven
wandering from the Nightly shore—
Tell me what thy lordly name is
on the Night's Plutonian shore!"
Quoth the raven, "Nevermore."

—Edgar Allan Poe

There comes Poe, with his raven,
like Barnaby Rudge,
Three-fifths of him genius,
and two-fifths sheer fudge.
Who talks like a book
of iambs and pentameters,
In a way to make people
of common sense damn metres,
Who has written some things
quite the best of their kind,
But the heart somehow seems all squeezed
out by the mind.

—James Russell Lowell

GOOD IDEA

"Give crayons. Adults are disturbingly impoverished of these magical dream sticks."

—Dr. SunWolf

HOME

"Home is the place where, when you have to go there, they have to take you in."

—Robert Frost

"Home life as we understand it is no more natural to us than a cage is natural to a cockatoo."

—George Bernard Shaw

"A house is not a home unless it contains food and fire for the mind as well as the body."

—Benjamin Franklin

"The difference between a house and a home is this: A house may fall down, but a home is broken up."

—Elbert Hubbard

"When I can no longer bear to think of the victims of broken homes, I begin to think of the victims of intact ones."

—Peter De Vries

"It may be that the satisfaction I need depends on my going away, so that when I've gone and come back, I'll find it at home."

—Rumi

"Television has brought back murder into the home...where it belongs."

—Alfred Hitchcock

"One of the oldest human needs is having someone to wonder where you are when you don't come home at night."

—**Margaret Mead**

TEACH YOUR CHILDREN...

"I am convinced that, except in a few extraordinary cases, one form or another of an unhappy childhood is essential to the formation of exceptional gifts."

—**Thornton Wilder**

CANNIBALS?

"Nothing more strongly arouses our disgust than cannibalism, yet we make the same impression on Buddhists and vegetarians, for we feed on babies, though not our own."

—**Robert Louis Stevenson**

A DAY AT THE BEACH

"The prospect of a long day at the beach makes me panic. There is no harder work I can think of than taking myself off to somewhere pleasant, where I am forced to stay for hours and 'have fun.'"

—**Phillip Lopate**

KNOCK FIVE TIMES

"Go to your bosom: Knock there, and ask your heart what it doth know."

—**William Shakespeare**

"How strange that nature does not knock, and yet does not intrude!"

—Emily Dickinson

"The traveler has to knock at every alien door to come to his own, and he has to wonder through all the outer worlds to reach the innermost shrine at the end."

—Rabindranath Tagore

"The best way to knock the chip off your neighbor's shoulder is to pat him on the back."

—Anonymous

I'm blastin', outlastin'
Colors like Shaft,
so you could say I'm shaftin'
Old English filled my mind
And I came up with a funky rhyme
I'm gonna knock you out (HUUUH!)
Mama said knock you out (HUUUH!)

—LL Cool J

ON WORDS

"Words today are like the shells and rope of seaweed which a child brings home glistening from the beach and which in an hour have lost their luster."

—Cyril Connolly

"A man thinks that by mouthing hard words he understands hard things."

—Herman Melville

"No one means all he says, and yet very few say all they mean, for words are slippery and thought is viscous."

—Henry Adams

"Words ought to be a little wild, for they are the assaults of thought on the unthinking."

—John Maynard Keynes

"If you would be pungent, be brief; for it is with words as with sunbeams. The more they are condensed, the deeper they burn."

—Robert Southey

"Words are a wonderful form of communication, but they will never replace kisses and punches."

—Ashleigh Brilliant

HMMM...

"It is of interest to note that while some dolphins are reported to have learned English—up to fifty words used in correct context—no human being has been reported to have learned dolphinese."

—Carl Sagan

MORE FISH STORIES

"Many men go fishing all of their lives without knowing it is not fish they are after."

—Henry David Thoreau

"All cats love fish but fear to wet their paws."

—Chinese proverb

"Give a man a fish and you feed him for a day. Teach a man to fish and you feed him for a lifetime."

—Anonymous

"Give a man a fish and you feed him for a day. Teach a man to fish and hopefully he learns before he starves to death."

—Anonymous

"Give a person a fish and you feed them for a day. Teach a person to use the Internet and they won't bother you for weeks."

—Anonymous

"Fish die belly upward, and rise to the surface. Its their way of falling."

—Andre Gide

HELL IS...

"Hell is other people."

—Jean-Paul Sartre

"Hell is paved with Good Samaritans."

—William Holden

"Hell is paved with priests' skulls."

—St. John Chrysostom

"The infliction of cruelty with a good conscience is a delight to moralists. That is why they invented hell."

—Bertrand Russell

"An intelligent hell would be better than a stupid paradise."

—Victor Hugo

"In hell there is no other punishment than to begin over and over again the tasks left unfinished in your lifetime."

—Andre Gide

"The safest road to hell is the gradual one—the gentle slope, soft underfoot, without sudden turnings, without milestones, without signposts."

—C. S. Lewis

"I don't like to commit myself about heaven and hell—you see, I have friends in both places."

—Mark Twain

"Eskimo: 'If I did not know about God and sin, would I go to hell?' Priest: 'No, not if you did not know.' Eskimo: 'Then why did you tell me?'"

—Annie Dillard

HEAVEN IS...

Earth's crammed with heaven,
And every common bush afire with God;
And only he who sees takes off his shoes;
The rest sit round it and pluck blackberries.

—Elizabeth Barrett Browning

"There are glimpses of heaven to us in every act, or thought, or word, that raises us above ourselves."

—Arthur P. Stanley

"Heaven will be no heaven to me if I do not meet my wife there."
—**Andrew Jackson**

"Heaven, heaven is a place, place where nothing, nothing ever happens."
—**David Byrne**

ALREADY GONE

"Who is staring at the sea is already sailing a little."
—**Paul Carvel**

PROGRESS?

"If the human race wants to go to hell in a basket, technology can help it get there by jet. It won't change the desire or the direction, but it can greatly speed the passage."
—**Charles M. Allen**

"Anything that is theoretically possible will be achieved in practice, no matter what the technical difficulties are, if it is desired greatly enough."
—**Arthur C. Clarke**

"By his very success in inventing labor-saving devices, modern man has manufactured an abyss of boredom that only the privileged class in earlier civilizations have ever fathomed."
—**Lewis Mumford**

"Technological progress is like an axe in the hands of a pathological criminal."
—**Albert Einstein**

"Man is an animal with primary instincts of survival. Consequently his ingenuity has developed first and his soul afterwards. The progress of science is far ahead of man's ethical behavior."

—Charlie Chaplin

"Advances in medicine and agriculture have saved vastly more lives than have been lost in all the wars in history."

—Carl Sagan

"The universe is full of magical things, patiently waiting for our wits to sharpen."

—Eden Phillpotts

"Do you realize if it weren't for Edison we'd be watching TV by candlelight?"

—Al Boliska

"The factory of the future will have only two employees, a man and a dog. The man will be there to feed the dog. The dog will be there to keep the man from touching the equipment."

—Warren G. Bennis

SMART MOUTH: WILLIAM JAMES

"If you believe that feeling bad or worrying long enough will change a past or future event, then you are residing on another planet with a different reality system."

"The deepest principle in human nature is the craving to be appreciated."

"Objective evidence and certitude are doubtless very fine ideals to play with, but where on this moonlit and dream-visited planet are they found?"

"It is well for the world that in most of us, by the age of thirty, the character has set like plaster, and will never soften again."

"The best argument I know for an immortal life is the existence of a man who deserves one."

"Great emergencies and crises show us how much greater our vital resources are than we had supposed."

"Everybody should do at least two things each day that he hates to do, just for practice."

HMMM...

"The sudden and abrupt deletion of all individuals occupying the lower bands of the Tone Scale from the social order would result in an almost instant rise in the cultural tone and would interrupt the dwindling spiral into which any society may have entered."

—L. Ron Hubbard

ON WALLS

"Reality doesn't impress me. I only believe in intoxication, in ecstasy, and when ordinary life shackles me, I escape, one way or another. No more walls."

—Anaïs Nin

"The walls are the publishers of the poor."

—Eduardo Galeano

"So Brother Matthew locked the gate behind me, and I was enclosed in the four walls of my new freedom."

—**Thomas Merton**

"The more enlightened our houses are, the more their walls ooze ghosts."

—**Italo Calvino**

"There are no boundaries in the real Planet Earth. No United States, no Russia, no China, no Taiwan. Rivers flow unimpeded across the swaths of continents. The persistent tides, the pulse of the sea do not discriminate; they push against all the varied shores on Earth."

—**Jacques Cousteau**

"We should thank God that he did not give us the power of hearing through walls; otherwise there would be no such thing as friendship."

—**Austin O'Malley**

FOREVER YOUNG

"Do not commit the error common among the young, of assuming that if you cannot save the whole of mankind you have failed."

—**Jan de Hartog**

"Memory is the Fountain of Youth, not the preserver of truth."

—**Peckeroy**

"If you want to recapture your youth, just cut off his allowance."

—**Al Bernstein**

"There is many a young cockerel that will stand upon a dunghill and crow about his father, by way of making his own plumage to shine."

—Elizabeth Gaskell

"Time misspent in youth is sometimes all the freedom one ever has."

—Anita Brookner

"It is an illusion that youth is happy, an illusion of those who have lost it."

—W. Somerset Maugham

"I remember my youth and the feeling that will never come back anymore—the feeling that I could last forever, outlast the sea, the earth, and all men; the deceitful feeling that lures us on to joys, to perils, to love, to vain effort—to death; the triumphant conviction of strength, the heat of life in the handful of dust, the glow in the heart that with every year grows dim, grows cold, grows small, and expires—and expires, too soon, too soon—before life itself."

—Joseph Conrad

"You are only young once, and if you work it right, once is enough."

—Joe E. Lewis

May your heart always be joyful
And may your song always be sung
May you stay forever young.

—Bob Dylan

HMMM...

"If I thought every day was a new start, I would kill myself. I would do so over and over again for as long as might prove necessary."

—Frank Kuppner

ON QUOTATIONS

"Most anthologists of quotations are like those who eat cherries or oysters: first picking the best ones and winding up by eating everything."

—Nicolas de Chamfort

"What is all wisdom save a collection of platitudes? Take fifty of our current proverbial sayings—they are so trite, so threadbare, that we can hardly bring our lips to utter them. Nonetheless they embody the concentrated experience of the race."

—Norman Douglas

"All maxims have their antagonist maxims; proverbs should be sold in pairs, a single one being but a half truth."

—William Mathews

"It is a good thing for an uneducated man to read books of quotations...The quotations when engraved upon the memory give you good thoughts. They also make you anxious to read the authors and look for more."

—Winston Churchill

"The ability to quote is a serviceable substitute for wit."

—W. Somerset Maugham

"The quoting of an aphorism, like the angry barking of a dog or the smell of overcooked broccoli, rarely indicates that something helpful is about to happen."

—Lemony Snicket

"The only way to read a book of aphorisms without being bored is to open it at random and, having found something that interests you, close the book and meditate."

—Prince de Ligne

"QUOTATION, n.: The act of repeating erroneously the words of another."

—Ambrose Bierce

ADVICE FOR PARENTS

"To all parents who ask me what my advice is to their boys' education, I always say: 'Let them learn foreign languages: French, Italian, German, Spanish, as many more as they can. The other things—the length of rivers, the accession of kings, the names of battles, even multiplication and subtraction—are negligible; but conversation with foreigners is vital.'"

—E. V. Lucas

THE HOLE WORLD

"A hole is nothing at all, but you can break your neck in it."

—Austin O'Malley

"The nation is prosperous on the whole, but how much prosperity is there in a hole?"

—Will Rogers

"Let your actions always speak for you, but be forever on guard against the terrible traps of false pride and conceit that can halt your progress. The next time you are tempted to boast, just place your fist in a full pail of water, and when you remove it, the hole remaining will give you a correct measure of your importance."

—Og Mandino

"The drops of rain make a hole in the stone, not by violence but by oft falling."

—Lucretius

"In a hole in the ground there lived a hobbit. Not a nasty, dirty, wet hole, filled with the ends of worms and an oozy smell, nor yet a dry, bare, sandy hole with nothing in it to sit down on or to eat: it was a hobbit-hole, and that means comfort."

—J. R. R. Tolkien

"Where you used to be, there is a hole in the world, which I find myself constantly walking around in the daytime, and falling in at night."

—Edna St. Vincent Millay

MEMORIES

Let the bucket of memory down into the well,
bring it up. Cool, cool minutes. No one
stirring, no plans. Just being there.

—William Stafford

WE CAN BE HEROES

"A hero is an ordinary individual who finds the strength to persevere and endure in spite of overwhelming obstacles."

—Christopher Reeve

"A hero is someone who understands the responsibility that comes with his freedom."

—Bob Dylan

"A hero is no braver than an ordinary man, but he is braver five minutes longer."

—Ralph Waldo Emerson

"Heroes are people who rise to the occasion and slip quietly away."

—Tom Brokaw

"A boy doesn't have to go to war to be a hero; he can say he doesn't like pie when he sees there isn't enough to go around."

—Edgar Watson Howe

"I'm a hero...with coward's legs."

—Spike Milligan

"True heroism is remarkably sober, very undramatic. It is not the urge to surpass all others at whatever cost, but the urge to serve others at whatever cost."

—Arthur Ashe

"You don't raise heroes, you raise sons. And if you treat them like sons, they'll turn out to be heroes, even if it's just in your own eyes."

—**Walter M. Schirra Sr.**

"My belt holds my pants up, but the belt loops hold my belt up. So which one's the real hero?"

—**Mitch Hedberg**

A FAILURE IS...

"A failure is a man who has blundered but is not able to cash in the experience."

—**Elbert Hubbard**

NEW WORDS

"Instead of forming new words I recommend to you any kind of artful management by which you may be able to give cost to old ones."

—**Horace**

"English is such a deliciously complex and undisciplined language, we can bend, fuse, distort words to all our purposes. We give old words new meanings, and we borrow new words from any language that intrudes into our intellectual environment."

—**Willard Gaylin**

"We can best help you to prevent war not by repeating your words and following your methods but by finding new words and creating new methods."

—Virginia Woolf

GOOD ADVICE

Folk wisdom makes it very clear
This truth for every soul;
However hard you wash your rear
You'll never make an eye from the hole.

—Igor Guberman

ON FLYING

"Why fly? Simple. I'm not happy unless there's some room between me and the ground."

—Richard Bach

"The desire to fly is an idea handed down to us by our ancestors who, in their grueling travels across trackless lands in prehistoric times, looked enviously on the birds soaring freely through space, at full speed, above all obstacles, on the infinite highway of the air."

—Wilbur Wright

"The airport runway is the most important main street in any town."

—Norm Crabtree

"You define a good flight by negatives: you didn't get hijacked, you didn't crash, you didn't throw up, you weren't late, you weren't nauseated by the food. So you are grateful."

—Paul Theroux

"When once you have tasted flight, you will forever walk the earth with your eyes turned skyward, for there you have been, and there you will always long to return."

—Leonardo da Vinci

"You haven't seen a tree until you've seen its shadow from the sky."

—Amelia Earhart

TIME SAVERS

"To choose time is to save time."

—Francis Bacon

"Perhaps the most important use of money—it saves time. Life is so short, and there's so much to do, one can't afford to waste a minute; and just think how much you waste, for instance, in walking from place to place instead of going by bus and in going by bus instead of by taxi."

—W. Somerset Maugham

"Time is an equal-opportunity employer. Each human being has exactly the same number of hours and minutes every day. Rich people can't buy more hours. Scientists can't invent new minutes. And you can't save time to spend it on another day. Even so, time is amazingly fair and forgiving. No matter how much time you've wasted in the past, you still have an entire tomorrow."

—Denis Waitely

"The advantage of taking an instant dislike to somebody is that it saves time."

—Spike Milligan

HMMM...

"Sponges grow in the ocean. That just kills me. I wonder how much deeper the ocean would be if that didn't happen."

—Steven Wright

SMART MOUTH: JULIA CHILD

"The only time to eat diet food is while you're waiting for the steak to cook."

"Noncooks think it's silly to invest two hours' work in two minutes' enjoyment; but if cooking is evanescent, well, so is the ballet."

"I was thirty-two when I started cooking; up until then, I just ate."

"Drama is very important in life: You have to come on with a bang. You never want to go out with a whimper."

"If you're afraid of butter, just use cream."

"How can a nation be called great if its bread tastes like Kleenex?"

"Life itself is the proper binge."

&%#$*&&!

"At no time is freedom of speech more precious than when a man hits his thumb with a hammer."

—Marshall Lumsden

CLOSING ARGUMENT

"Even in a time of elephantine vanity and greed, one never has to look far to see the campfires of gentle people. Lacking any other purpose in life, it would be good enough to live for their sake."

—Garrison Keillor

INDEXES